ARNHEM
1944 BATTLE STORY

CHRIS BROWN

The History Press

This book is dedicated to the memory of my late father-in-law, Robert
Smith of Arran and to his dear friend James 'Laindon' Jackson Cornwell,
who died in Japanese captivity on or about
3 May 1943, aged twenty-two.

First published 2011
This paperback edition first published 2022

The History Press
97 St George's Place, Cheltenham,
Gloucestershire, GL50 3QB
www.thehistorypress.co.uk

British Library Cataloguing in Publication Data.
A catalogue record for this book is available from the British Library.

ISBN 978 1 80399 024 8

Typesetting and origination by The History Press
Printed and bound in Great Britain by TJ Books Limited, Padstow, Cornwall.

MIX
Paper from
responsible sources
FSC® C013056

Trees for LYfe

CONTENTS

ACKNOWLEDGEMENTS

As ever I am indebted to my wife and I am grateful for the patience of my children and their partners, Robert, Charis, Christopher, Colin, Alex, Juliet and Mariola and my dog Sam, all of whom have to listen to much more history than can possibly be reasonable. My grateful thanks also to the series editor, Jo de Vries, whose patience with writers is seemingly boundless and also to Ian Davidson of the Parachute and Glider Warfare Group and Mark Hickman at the Pegasus Archive for all their generous help with the photographs. Lloyd Clark kindly granted permission for use and adaptation of several maps from his excellent book, *Arnhem: Operation Market Garden, September 1944* (Sutton/The History Press, 2002). Several photographs have also been used from the recent detailed study, *Operation Market Garden: Legend of the Waal Crossing* (The History Press, 2011), by kind permission of the author, Tim Lynch.

LIST OF ILLUSTRATIONS

Unless otherwise credited all illustrations have been sourced from US and UK public domain sources.

List of Illustrations

Arnhem 1944

INTRODUCTION

The Market Garden operation, and particularly the battle that raged in and around Arnhem and Oosterbeek for nine days in September 1944, has attracted a remarkable amount of attention and a formidable amount of material has been published about it, by participants and by both popular and academic historians. There are many reasons why it has proved to be such a 'popular' battle. It was an unparalleled event; by far the greatest airborne operation there had ever been. It was dramatic and innovative, and it captured the imagination of the public throughout Europe and the United States. It has that special aura of a romantic and, in a sense, glorious defeat.

Another reason that it has been of enduring interest is that it is very rare to be able to study a divisional battle in such isolation. The battle area is relatively small and can be studied on the ground to a worthwhile degree in a fairly short space of time. For anyone who has the opportunity to visit the city of Arnhem and town of Oosterbeek, I can thoroughly recommend Major John Waddy's book *A Tour of the Battlefields of Arnhem,* and also Major and Mrs Holt's *Battlefield Guide to Operation Market Garden* for those who wish to see the bigger picture of the campaign as a whole.

Although this book is focused on the struggle of the British 1st Airborne Division and the attached 1st Polish Parachute Brigade, it is important to remember that their fight was part of a much larger offensive; there would have been no strategic value in capturing what is now called the John Frost Bridge over the Lower Rhine without also gaining control of a chain of river crossings from Neerpelt to Nijmegen.

Perhaps the single most important factor which has kept the battle alive in the public consciousness is the remarkable courage exhibited by so many men in such a short space of time and in such a small area. To some extent echoes of the events at Arnhem have drowned out examples of outstanding soldiering in other parts of the campaign. The 82nd and 101st Airborne divisions of the United States Army carried out their tasks with stupendous vigour and professional ability, and with many acts of astonishing courage. The assault at Nijmegen is one example; soldiers of Colonel Reuben Tucker's 504th Parachute Infantry Regiment boarded boats that they had never seen before and undertook an attack of a kind that they had never been trained for under heavy fire and in broad daylight. This outstanding feat of arms is, rightly, a famed example of exceptional courage and tenacity, but it has, perhaps, overshadowed the determination and achievements of the other elements of the US Airborne divisions. It is somehow typical of the entire Market Garden operation that once the 504th had stormed the bridge and the British armour had crossed it, the day's operations ground to a halt.

If the Market Garden offensive – and the Arnhem battle in particular – is a tale of bravery and ability in a particularly trying military environment, it is also a tale of confusion, professional incompetence and eventual failure in which sheer common-or-garden bad luck played a conspicuous part. It is a little bit too easy to point the finger at several senior commanders for a mixture of slap-dash work and wishful thinking. It does no harm to remember Clausewitz's (the famous military theorist) warning that the things required to achieve victory in war are very simple, but that in war even the very simplest things are exceptionally difficult to achieve and, of course, the old military dictum that 'no plan survives contact with the enemy'.

Introduction

It is impossible to escape the conclusion that Allied officers at all senior levels – British and American, army and air force – failed to really take account of the enemy. Of the senior officers briefed before the landings only two – General Sosabowski and Brigadier Hackett – seem to have been at all concerned about the possibility that the German Army might have some influence on the progress of the operation.

For the Germans, Arnhem was really the last battlefield victory in the western theatre. If the military environment was challenging for the Allies, it was no less so for the Germans. They had to overcome the confusion of a long retreat in front of an enemy with massive air superiority, and at a time when their ability to replace men and material had been overstrained for years. Few could have been in any doubt that they were in the course of losing the war, but they were not yet ready to give up the struggle.

Although the troops of the main body of the German Army at Arnhem – 9th and 10th divisions of General Bittrich's 2nd SS Panzer Corps – had had some training in anti-airborne operations in 1943, the majority of those divisions were dead, wounded or prisoners by September 1944. Many of the troops who fought the British at Arnhem were not highly trained, experienced and motivated troops, but army and SS trainees or sailors and airmen waiting for re-assignment and re-training. The shock of being handed a rifle and a few rounds of ammunition before being thrown into the battle – often under officers and NCOs that they did not know – must have been dreadful. The fact that they were able to withstand an enormous onslaught on the ground and in the air, and not only contain, but defeat, a body of troops like the 1st Airborne Division is a testament to astonishingly good staff work, and to the training and commitment of the ordinary German soldier. That they did so with courage and a considerable degree of humanity – and in several incidents chivalry – is all the more remarkable.

TIMELINE

1940

10/11 May	German glider troops seize the Belgian fort of Eben-Emael in the first airborne operation in Western Europe, inspiring Churchill to order the formation of an airborne force to total 5,000 men
22 June	No. 2 Commando is assigned to a parachute and glider role
22 November	No. 2 Commando is re-named 11th Special Air Service Battalion and becomes the foundation of British airborne forces
	1st Parachute Brigade and 1st Airlanding Brigade are formed as the basis of 1st Airborne Division under the command of Lieutenant General Browning

1941

10 February	The first British airborne venture, Operation Colossus, is mounted to seize and destroy an aqueduct in Calibri, southern Italy. The operation fails to achieve its objective
27/28 February	Operation Biting is mounted to capture German radar equipment at Bruneval and is a success

Timeline

1941	September	Formation of 1st Polish Parachute Brigade at Leven, Scotland under Major General Sosabowski. The Poles invented and developed many techniques and practices which had a profound effect on the development of Allied airborne forces. The brigade was initially raised for operations in Poland in support of the Polish Government in exile
	10 October	1st Airlanding Brigade formed under Brigadier Hopkinson
1942	November	1st Parachute Brigade and other elements of 1st Airborne Division are deployed to North Africa. Units are in action between 12 and 29 November at Bone, Beja, Souk-el-Akra and Pont du Fahs
1943	July	Elements of the airborne forces are deployed in Operation Husky, the invasion of Sicily. Towards the end of the year 1st Airborne units are withdrawn to Britain to train for the invasion of North-west Europe
1944	January	Major General Urquhart takes command of 1st Airborne Division
	June	A plan to land 1st Airborne near Caen as part of the Normandy campaign is abandoned due to the risk of high losses. Over the next two months at least a dozen proposed operations were abandoned either because they were unfeasible or because the advance to the Seine was so rapid that the planned objectives were overrun before the operation could be mounted
	19–25 August	The battle and liberation of Paris
	1 September	Eisenhower assumes command of all Allied forces in Europe, superseding Montgomery

Arnhem 1944

2 September   Allied troops enter Belgium

3 September   British Second Army liberates Brussels

4 September   Montgomery is given control of 1st Allied
                        Airborne Army and starts to formulate a plan
                        to renew the offensive in North-west Europe

7 September   11th Armoured Division crosses the
                        Albert Canal

10 September   Eisenhower accepts Montgomery's
                        ambitious plan for a massive airborne
                        operation to seize the road from Neerpelt
                        to Arnhem – Operation Market Garden

11 September   15th Scottish Division crosses into the
                        Netherlands

16 September   Air strikes in support of Market Garden
                        begin throughout the Arnhem–Nijmegen–
                        Eindhoven–Grave areas

17 September   First lift of the British 1st Airborne Division
                        lands at Arnhem as the American 101st
                        and 82nd Airborne divisions land around
                        Nijmegen and Eindhoven

18 September   The second lifts of the three airborne
                        divisions arrive

19 September   Poor weather conditions in Britain prevent
                        the deployment of the infantry battalions of
                        1st Polish Parachute Brigade

20 September   Nijmegen Bridge is captured by 504th
                        Parachute Infantry Regiment

21 September   The infantry battalions of 1st Polish Parachute
                        Brigade are dropped around Driel on the
                        south side of the Lower Rhine. Arnhem Bridge
                        is recovered by the Germans

24 September   Lieutenant General Horrocks' XXX Corps
                        reaches the Lower Rhine

25 September   Horrocks and Browning agree that Market
                        Garden should be abandoned and 1st
                        Airborne is withdrawn from Oosterbeek
                        through the night

1944

HISTORICAL
BACKGROUND

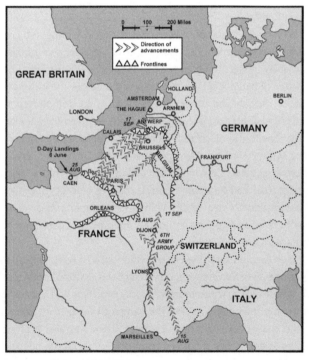

1. North-west Europe, 1944. (Courtesy of Lloyd Clark, Arnhem)

The Normandy landings of 6 June 1944 opened a new front in the war against Nazi Germany. As a consequence of a thorough deception campaign, the Germans were taken completely by surprise, indeed for some weeks Hitler persisted in believing that the Normandy landings were no more than a deception and that the main Allied effort would be made at Calais. The initial landings were very successful and the Allied armies were firmly ensconced within days; however, the Germans reacted with incredible efficiency and the battle stalled at Caen, leading to a fierce struggle in the bocage of Normandy instead of a rapid breakout into the more open countryside of western France. Eventually the heavy losses in Normandy and the dramatic thrust of American armies from the Cotentin peninsula caused a collapse of the German defence, trapping a huge portion of the combat strength of German Army Group B at Falaise.

The loss of thousands of Wehrmacht and SS troops, and great quantities of equipment, destabilised German strategy, compromising their ability to react to US and British operations. This was not simply a matter of battlefield losses. In the months before the Normandy invasion British and American air strikes had demolished the transport infrastructure that the Germans required to move new formations to the Normandy front and to replenish the units that were already engaged. Allied commanders had expected a rather different schedule. Capturing Caen had been a much more difficult project than had been anticipated, and had held up operations to a considerable degree, but neither Montgomery, who was the senior commander on the ground, nor his superior, Eisenhower had envisaged a German collapse.

When Brussels fell to the British divisions of 21st Army Group (the parent group of Second Army), they had been in action continuously for almost exactly three months. Supply problems and exhaustion were now major factors and the campaign faltered. In addition to the challenges faced by the armies, there was also profound disagreement among the Allied commanders about the next step. Eisenhower took the view that the general strategy should be to pressure the enemy on a broad front. British historians have taken this to mean a front hundreds of miles long, from the channel to the south of France. This was not at all what he had in mind. As long as Patton and Devers were making good progress and destroying the enemy, Eisenhower was reluctant to bring their operations to a dead halt, but on the other hand, so long as the British and Canadian armies were making similar progress in the north, he was not eager to interrupt them in their pursuit of an enemy who, in July and August, was looking like it might collapse completely, allowing a rapid advance into Germany. Equally, he was aware that the logistical effort available was not up to the task of supporting all of the Allied armies at the rates of advance that had occured during July and August.

Two influential figures were unhappy about the situation. Montgomery and Patton both believed that the Germans were on the verge of a total strategic and tactical breakdown and that one axis of advance with all of the resources of the Allies firmly behind it would knock Germany out of the war much more quickly than a combination of advances. Naturally, each believed that they were the man for the job and that his force was better suited for a major strategic strike into Germany.

What was not in question was that some action was needed. If the Germans were reeling under the blows they had already received, the last thing that was wanted was to allow them any opportunity to recover. Both men had valid points, but on balance, Eisenhower decided that Montgomery should have priority over Patton and that he should mount a major new offensive which would carry Allied forces though the Netherlands, across the remaining geographical barriers facing the northern army group: the rivers of Waal, Maas and Rhine, and on into Germany. Montgomery's forces would thus bypass the heavily fortified Siegfried Line, then move into the industrial heartland of Germany. In order to achieve this objective, Montgomery was given command of the three divisions of 1st Airborne Corps from the newly named 1st Airborne Army.

The Airborne Army had been formed partly as a means of avoiding unnecessary duplication of effort in the way of research and development, training and planning facilities, but chiefly to ensure the efficient use of the limited airlift capacity. It consisted of six divisions: British 1st Airborne, the American 82nd, 101st and 17th Airborne, the Scottish 52nd (Airportable) Division and the Polish Parachute Brigade. The 1st, 82nd and 101st divisions and the Polish Brigade would be available for the initial strike, with the 52nd standing by for delivery to the battlefield once Deelen airfield had been secured. The commanding officer of the Airborne Army was Lieutenant General Lewis Brereton, an American Army Air Force general, who had previously had command of the US 9th Air Force. The normal practice for joint American-British formations was to appoint an American officer as commander with a British officer as his deputy. That post was held by General Frederick Browning, known throughout the British Army as 'Boy' Browning. As Brereton's deputy and commander of the 1st Airborne Corps, Browning would be the commander of the airborne element of the operation that Montgomery intended to launch to renew the campaign.

The operation, codenamed 'Market Garden', would involve placing three divisions of airborne troops – more than 30,000 men and hundreds of vehicles and artillery pieces – at several locations behind the German lines; in the case of British 1st Airborne and the Polish Brigade almost 62 miles (100km) beyond the front. Over the next 24 hours – or 48 hours at most – General Horrocks' XXX Corps from General Dempsey's Second Army would advance from Neerpelt with extensive close air support and batter their way along one road, linking up with elements of 82nd and 101st Airborne divisions who would have seized and held a chain of bridges up to and including the great road bridge at Nijmegen; from there XXX Corps would press on to Arnhem and then on towards Germany.

If everything went to plan, the war would be over by the end of 1944. Most, if not all, of Germany would have fallen to the Allies; an achievement which would have implications for the future relationship between the Western Allies and the Soviet Union. At best this was an optimistic view of the situation, but there was something of an undercurrent of wishful thinking which pervaded

2. Elements of XXX Corps approaching the Meuse-Escaut Canal from the bridgehead at Neerpelt.

Allied planning and policy generally. The advance through France and Belgium had led to an assumption that the German Army was ready to crack and that one more great strategic victory would do the job; the collapse of the Wehrmacht and the SS, and the capture of the industrial regions of western Germany, would destroy whatever hope still existed among the German people and would bring about the final destruction of the Nazi's domestic political credibility. However attractive this may have seemed to elements in the Allied High Command it was far from being a realistic appreciation of the political, economic, strategic and tactical realities of the day.

Most importantly, it took no real account of the abilities of the German military. The fall of France seems to have been taken by some as an indication of things to come. Given the Allied experience of fighting the Germans this is something of a curiosity. The advance through Italy had been a costly and challenging business and was by no means complete in September 1944. The Germans had demonstrated time and again a remarkable capacity for reorganisation under difficult circumstances.

21

Clearly the Market Garden operation was a major risk, but the possible gains were commensurately great. The Germans had been in headlong retreat for weeks, culminating in the event that Netherlanders called 'Mad Tuesday'. On 5 September a host of German units and stray individuals streamed across the Netherlands heading for Germany with all the speed they could muster and little sign of any sort of order. This had been reported to Allied intelligence and taken very much to heart as an indication of the state of the enemy's forces. There was an argument to be made that a major strategic intervention with fresh troops might be able to take advantage of the German retreat and bolster the wider campaign.

Market Garden did not represent a change of policy on the part of either Montgomery or Eisenhower, merely a shift of emphasis. The ground campaign could have continued in the form that had been so successful since the breakout from Normandy had it not been for the growing exhaustion of Second Army. If the advance to Germany was to regain the momentum that the Allies had enjoyed over the preceding months there would have to be a major addition to the forces available. The only strategic reserve available to the Allies was the collection of airborne formations still based in the UK and, in truth, the fastest way to get them into the battle was to airlift them.

A major airborne deployment was not an unreasonable proposition in itself; what was the value of such a force if it was not to be used to intervene in the wider struggle? Even accepting that the fastest means of getting the airborne formations to the battle area was by air, it could be argued that dropping them in the midst of the enemy may not have been the best option. If the airlift capacity existed to take them to battle, it would have been just as easy to transport them to airfields in northern France and then move them to the front by road. There are two major flaws to this argument. The first would have been the challenge of transport control. The roads leading to the Netherlands were very heavily overcrowded by the demands of the armies already in action. Secondly, where were the thousands of necessary trucks to come from? Even if these issues could be overcome, there would have been the vast administrative

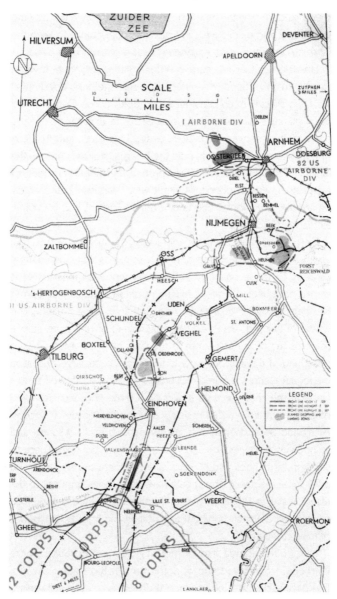

3. Map of the Market Garden operation. (Courtesy of Tim Lynch)

challenge of passing the new formations through to the front; by the time the airborne units were in action the opportunity to keep the Germans in a state of disorganised retreat might well have passed.

The Market Garden plan was formulated in just one week starting from 10 September 1944; however, the basic operational plan had already been considered. An operation – Comet – had been planned for distributing one airborne division across the main river crossings – Nijmegen, Grave, Eindhoven and Arnhem. The parachute forces would hold the bridges until such time as the tanks and infantry of XXX Corps pushed through. A great deal of the planning already done for Comet, which was itself based largely on another abandoned operation entitled 'Fifteen', was applicable to Market Garden.

Despite the plans being broadly similar, the strategic and tactical environment was not and although that was not immediately obvious to those concerned, there is a good argument that it should have been. The most significant difference was that Comet had been designed to take advantage of an existing situation. The whole of Second Army had been rapidly advancing since before the crossing of the Seine, but in the days before Market Garden the speed of the advance slowed to a snail's pace, largely because the logistical effort required was unsustainable. The other difference was that the enemy was no longer on the run. The Germans were offering more committed resistance which slowed down Second Army, and Second Army was also being held back by supply and manpower shortages. This afforded a little more breathing space to German formations, which in turn allowed them to reorganise and offer stiffer resistance. This should have been more apparent to the planning staff at Montgomery's and Browning's headquarters since it was most definitely apparent to battalion and brigade intelligence officers at the front.

It has been argued that Comet might have succeeded where Market Garden failed; the operation might have gone ahead a few days earlier, at a point when the Germans were still reeling. Success would have depended on the German Army throughout

Historical Background

Belgium and the Netherlands collapsing under one final blow – a straw breaking a camel's back. This is not a realistic analysis for a number of reasons. Chiefly, the German Army was in a rather better condition than the planners realised. Mad Tuesday notwithstanding, the crisis was, if not past, then certainly past its worst and German formations were beginning to get a grip on the situation. Moreover, the force to be committed was very much smaller. Only one brigade would be available for each of the operational areas and, apart from Arnhem, each area would contain more than one objective. Even if the objectives had all been taken with little loss, the force available to retain them would have been terribly vulnerable to counterattack. Furthermore, XXX Corps would have had even less time to replenish units and stockpile the fuel and ammunition required to advance 62 miles (100km).

There was also the question of the German reaction. Superficially it might seem that closing the bridges would prevent the German Army from retreating into the Netherlands and thus bring about a wholesale surrender of units trapped with the west banks of the Rhine, Meuse and Waal behind them and the onset of Second Army in front of them. However it is likely that Comet would have had quite the opposite effect. A threat to their only avenue of escape might well have persuaded German troops still in, or close to, contact with the enemy that it was in their better interests to fight hard and delay the British while units in the rear dealt with the slender parachute forces, thus securing the bridges for a continued withdrawal to Germany.

Even if Comet was mounted successfully the prospect that the Germans could be defeated in the Netherlands was a rather hopeful assumption in itself. There was no guarantee that the German High Command would prove incapable of mounting a determined resistance once the Allies had crossed the Rhine. It is true that the advance across Germany in the spring of 1945 was rapid and successful, but the situation was very different from that of the late summer and autumn of 1944. By 1945 the Germans had, to coin a phrase, 'shot their bolt' in the Ardennes offensive.

Market Garden was very much in the mould of Comet; the rationale behind the operation was identical and the forces were similar in form, though, of course, very much larger. A good deal has been made of the difficulties of mounting the operation in such a short space of time and there is some truth in this, however neither Comet nor Market Garden were planned in isolation; in fact some documents for Comet were recycled for its successor, the word Comet being obliterated by having Market Garden stamped over the top of the original title.

A succession of at least a dozen proposed operations had been cancelled before Comet, either because they had been deemed impractical or because the advance of the ground forces had proceeded more quickly than expected and had made the operations redundant. Inevitably this had had a damaging effect on the morale of the individual units of all of the airborne divisions, though probably more on the British than the American formations. The Americans had been in action in Normandy, whereas 1st Airborne had never seen action as a division at all, though several of the battalions had fought in North Africa or Italy. Even so, the divisional staff had been in place for some time and given all of the operations that they had planned for – though cancelled one and all – in theory at least, by September 1944 the planning process should have been honed to a very sharp edge indeed.

THE ARMIES

Responsibility for the execution of Market Garden and the Arnhem battle must rest with the commanders, as is the case for all battles. Eisenhower, Montgomery, Browning and Urquhart all made errors of judgement, each in his degree. With the benefit of hindsight it is all too easy to criticise a certain lack of focus and an unrealistic degree of optimism on the part of any one of them, and all of them in combination; however, there were many pressures on these officers, and we must bear in mind that an opportunity recognised and a moment seized can bring about huge success in war. Montgomery saw the opportunity and persuaded Eisenhower to back him. Browning accepted his mission and persuaded Urquhart to put up with a most unsatisfactory set of circumstances. Urquhart failed to ensure that his division was ready to fight a divisional battle and managed to become separated from his headquarters at the very point when he could have made a difference to the shape of the battle.

A number of historians when criticising the Market Garden operation have neglected – or have chosen to ignore – the fact that not all of these officers had much, if any, practical experience of airborne warfare on the scale proposed for Market Garden. Parachute and glider troops had been committed in the Mediterranean theatre and in the Normandy invasion, but the

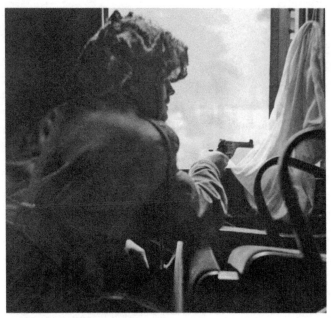

4. British officer armed only with a service revolver.

situations had been very different. The North African and Italian operations had been relatively small affairs, and although airborne troops had been used extensively in Normandy, it was as part of a mammoth operation which had been months in the planning. Although Market Garden was, in essence, a much larger version of Comet, and although some of the planning aspects remained the same, there was very little time to examine the myriad details which make the difference to success or failure.

Eisenhower and Montgomery – quite reasonably – expected to be able to rely on the professional ability of their subordinates, particularly those who would have operational responsibility. As head of the 1st Airborne Corps, Browning was responsible for the troops once they got on the ground, but the airlift aspect of the operation was almost entirely in the hands of Air Force staffs whose appreciation of the priorities of the combat units was extremely limited. From the earliest stage of planning General Brereton insisted on a daylight drop, in part at least because many of the American aircrews involved had had very little training in night operations. This was accepted, albeit reluctantly, by the three divisional commanders, though a dawn drop would have had many advantages. Once the airlift plan was established, Brereton was unwilling to consider any changes, and this was a major problem. All of the airborne commanders sought to make alterations to their proposed drop zones for a variety of reasons, but none could convince Brereton of their proposals. The air effort as a whole suffered from a lack of flexibility and from divided responsibilities. Although the delivery of 1st Airborne to Arnhem was Brereton's province, re-supply was largely a British affair, and all transport requests had to be referred to Air Marshal Leigh Mallory. This was an area in which the British had a considerable degree of expertise; several major operations in Burma had relied on air transport to supply ground forces on a similar scale; however, failures in communications, equipment and liaison between air and ground forces would make supply a critical issue at Arnhem.

The British

The formation of parachute units in the British Army was one of Winston Churchill's initiatives. Impressed by the success of the German attack on the Netherlands fortress of Eben Emael in 1940, Churchill ordered the creation of an airborne force. Initially the project was combined with the development of the new Commando force and training was under way by July. There was some support for the project in army circles, but preparations for a German invasion across the channel naturally took precedence. The RAF was rather less keen, and was, at times, positively obstructive. By the end of 1940 the parachute force, now known as 11th Special Air Service had come into being, but was not yet up to battalion strength. The project grew in stature over the next six months and by the late summer of 1941 plans had been made to raise a brigade of four battalions with a specialist engineering unit, and augmented by a second brigade group of glider troops. By the end of the year the airborne element had become a notional division, with General Browning at its head.

Browning was well acquainted with the vagaries of dealing with government departments, but had very little operational experience of any kind. The first action of the airborne force was carried out in February 1942. A company of the 2nd Battalion, commanded by Major John Frost, was dropped in France to make a raid on the Bruneval radar installation – partly to put it out of commission, partly to acquire German radar technology. The raid was successful despite the fact that a number of men were dropped far from the target area.

By November 1942 the three battalions of 1st Parachute Brigade had been sent to North Africa and three drops were made with limited success. Two more airborne operations – one with the glider troops of 1st Airlanding Brigade – were mounted during the campaign in Sicily in the summer of 1943. The men were transported in Waco gliders that they had not even seen, let alone trained in, the

5. Four of these American Waco gliders were assigned to the Arnhem operation to transport American air support control staff.

weather conditions were unsuitable and less than 10 per cent of the gliders actually got as far as the target area; more than half of them ditched in the sea with appalling loss of life. Three days later, on 13 July, 1st Parachute Brigade was dispatched to take the Primasole Bridge. Less than one third of the men and only four of the gliders carrying their heavier equipment were delivered on target. The bridge was taken, but lost shortly thereafter and then regained when ground troops arrived with tanks.

Overall, the venture into airborne operations had not been a howling success, though largely because of factors beyond the control of the parachute forces themselves. These were chiefly the weather, poor training of aircrew and the reluctance of air force officers to really engage with the needs of the operations when it came to choosing drop zones (DZs) and landing zones (LZs), but above all a very limited understanding among senior commanders about the practicalities and limitations of airborne warfare.

A lack of clear-cut tactical successes on the ground was compounded by a lack of interest and, in some cases, hostility to further development of the airborne arm. The RAF was not enchanted with the idea, believing that parachute and glider operations were an unnecessary drain on their resources. Although there was still a degree of support in the army hierarchy, there was increasing opposition in some quarters. The Parachute Regiment needed volunteers, and recruiting parties passed through virtually every part of the army in Britain and overseas looking for suitable candidates. Naturally these tended to be highly motivated individuals and their loss was sorely felt. Additionally, the airborne formations spent a great deal of time in training or on standby for operations that never came to fruition, which led to a fall in morale and men requesting transfers back to their original regiments, making jokes about how they had joined a formation that was not so much 'airborne' as 'stillborn'.

A second division (6th Airborne) was formed in 1943 and various additions to the existing airborne arsenal were examined, even to the extent of a specially designed light tank – the Tetrarch – which could be landed by glider. By 1944 the airborne arm had become an enormous drain on the resources of the Allies. Between the two British and three American airborne divisions, the 52nd Airportable Division and the Polish Parachute Brigade, it consisted of rather more than 60,000 men and literally thousands of trucks and artillery pieces, not to mention the thousands of aircraft, millions of man hours and vast amounts of fuel that would be needed to actually airlift them into battle.

The Airborne Army was far too large an investment to be allowed to sit on the shelf. The three airborne divisions that had been dropped in Normandy had made a positive impact on the battle, despite some units being very badly scattered, and captured the imagination of both the public and the military establishment. By September the American 82nd and 101st divisions and the British 1st Airborne were considered ready for battle. This was certainly the case for the American formations; they had gained valuable experience in Normandy, particularly in regard to fighting as formations rather than individual units, and were now well rested, confident, commanded by men who understood the nature of airborne warfare and the replacements for men lost in combat had been thoroughly integrated.

This was not really the case for 1st Airborne. The heavy losses in Africa and Italy had been made good, but a very large proportion of the new men had little or no experience of battle, the division had been 'milked' to provide officers for the new 6th Airborne Division and the divisional commander, General Urquhart, had only been in place since January. It probably did not help that he had been installed over the head of Brigadier Lathbury, who had been told that he would get command of the division as his predecessor, General Down, was being posted to the Far East to raise an Indian Parachute formation.

R.E. Urquhart

Born on 28 November 1902, Urquhart was commissioned into the Highland Light Infantry in 1920 and served in Malta beside the actor David Niven, who described Urquhart as a 'serious soldier of great charm'. He served in India in the early part of the war until posted back to Britain in 1941 as a staff officer in 3rd Division. He was promoted to lieutenant colonel and was appointed commander of the Duke of Cornwall's Light Infantry for a short time before joining the staff of 51st Highland Division in North Africa. He took command of 231st Brigade in 50th Northumberland Division and commanded the brigade during the landings and subsequent operations in Sicily.

After a period of service as the senior staff officer to XII Corps he was promoted to major general and given command of 1st Airborne Division early in 1944. Despite being something of an 'outsider' and the fact that he was forced to take several weeks sick leave due to a bout of malaria, he was able to gain respect and affection from the division by the time of the Market Garden operation in September. The division saw no further action in the war and by 1950 Urquhart had taken on a very different command role as General Officer Commanding of Malaya Command during the fight against the Communist insurgents. He returned to the UK in 1952 to take command of 16th Airborne Division, a Territorial formation. He left the army in 1955 and made a successful career in industry, retiring in 1970.

6. General Urquhart outside his headquarters at the Hartenstein Hotel in Oosterbeek. The hotel now houses an excellent museum dedicated to the battle.

Rationally, Lathbury was the obvious choice. He had commanded 3rd Battalion from its inception and had led 1st Brigade in Italy. Urquhart was selected for two reasons. When Browning was told that he would be getting a replacement for Downs from outside the airborne family he only asked that the officer should be 'hot from the battle'; a laudable attitude, and Urquhart had made a fine job of leading a brigade in the desert, but a more important factor in his appointment was that he was a protégé of Montgomery.

Even so, he had managed to make a good impression in a formation which rather saw itself as a self-contained organism separate from the army as a whole. Despite coming down with a bout of malaria which put him out of action for three weeks and doubtless impaired his stamina for several more, Urquhart soon became a fixture, popular throughout the division. He clearly did his level best to offset his inexperience with sheer hard work, but he was hampered in his efforts to ensure that his command was in the best possible shape. In the eight months before he took his command to battle he had to spend a great deal of time at conferences and meetings. The majority of these were in London, far from his headquarters and time consuming to reach since he was prone to airsickness and chose to travel by road.

His lack of airborne experience put him at a disadvantage in several respects when it came to planning operations. Urquhart, although conscious of the need to have his force delivered as close to the objectives as possible, was relatively junior and was not sufficiently sure of himself to be able to press his case with his superiors. The same applied to his relationship with his subordinates. All of the brigade and unit commanders had been in their posts for some time and as a newcomer Urquhart probably did not press them hard enough in the key areas of brigade and divisional training. Only one full-scale divisional exercise – Rags – was held before Market Garden. Although useful lessons were learnt, Rags was of limited value. The exercise was conducted in May and the division was deployed, not from the skies, but from trucks, so many of the possible difficulties likely to be faced by an airborne division in combat simply were not addressed. Most importantly, the division was deployed as a whole so there was no question of having to deal with problems arising from the failure of elements to arrive in the right place or at the right time.

There were several causes of tensions within 1st Airborne – some units had suffered from repeated bouts of indiscipline, particularly the tendency for soldiers to 'go absent' by overstaying their leave. The vast majority had no intention of avoiding battle; they simply came to doubt that the endless chain of training and abandoned operations would ever result in the formation going into action. There were also some issues over the chain of command and there were problems about detailed planning. The various headquarters involved lay some distance apart and most of the issues were things that could not be explored on the telephone for obvious reasons of security, though in fact the most critical aspects of the operation – where and when the troops were to be delivered – had already been decided by General Brereton's staff and were not open to discussion anyway.

All the same, when Urquhart briefed his officers on 15 September the division was eager to get into the battle, though the divisional plan was, at best, questionable. This was particularly obvious in relation to the main target. Lathbury's 1st Brigade was to drop nearly 6.2 miles (10km) from the bridge, but – as Frost points out – the

> … advantageous characteristic of airborne troops is that they can be put on both sides of an obstacle before the battle commences, yet now that this was paramount, the air forces still would not conform.
>
> John Frost, *A Drop Too Many*

Attacks on both ends of the target and with as much surprise as possible is particularly important in an assault to take a bridge. Tactically, the problem is almost identical to that of approaching any valley or pass; the attackers must, at some point, make an assault into a very constricted area. The defenders can hardly fail to be aware of exactly where the attackers must make their move and can make their dispositions accordingly. A bridge is actually more difficult than a valley in that there is no scope whatsoever for the attackers to gain a position of advantage on the high ground that forms the flanks of the target.

The air staff had not been willing to budge on the question of dropping 1st Parachute Brigade, or even a portion of it, right beside the bridge. Realistically, Lathbury could not hope to have his men on the bridge in anything less than 3 hours even if they met absolutely no opposition. Clearly the Germans were not going to let that much time elapse before reacting and the objective would be painfully obvious as soon as the division appeared. Urquhart decided to use two of the three troops of his only mobile unit, 1st Parachute Reconnaissance Squadron, as a *coup de main* force. The squadron would unload their jeeps and move as quickly as possible to the bridge, secure it and wait for the arrival of the infantry battalions.

The brigade plan assigned one battalion and a troop of anti-tank guns to each of the three routes: Lion, Tiger and Leopard. Genuine surprise was obviously out of the question – by the time the infantry marched onto the bridge the Germans would have been aware of the operation for some hours, so Lathbury had to get his battalions into the town as quickly as possible. By using three routes he hoped that at least one would be reasonably free from German interference, and that the other two could be abandoned if necessary and, if so, that those two battalions could be moved onto the better route. On the other hand, the plan meant that none of the three battalion columns would have the strength to force a passage against a determined defence on any scale. A single company – or even less – if handled efficiently, might easily force any of the advancing battalions to alter their route and impose a lengthy delay while the small and vulnerable Reconnaissance Squadron, probably no more than a hundred men at best, would have to face whatever forces the Germans could commit to the bridge.

It would seem that none of the battalion commanders were very happy about their roles. The timescale left little opportunity for detailed battalion planning, though the quality of the soldiers and of unit training perhaps made this less significant than would normally be the case. More importantly, the brigade had too many secondary objectives. Only about half of the infantry strength of the division would land on 17 September, and more than half of those men would be required to secure and retain the drop zones and landing zones for 4th Parachute Brigade and the balance of the divisional assets.

This was the responsibility of Brigadier Hicks' 1st Airlanding Brigade. His force was rather stronger than Lathbury's brigade in a number of respects. Each of his battalions had four rifle companies instead of three, though half of the 2nd Battalion South Staffordshires would not arrive until the second lift due to the shortage of aircraft and gliders. The Airlanding units each had two integral anti-tank platoons giving them each eight 6 pounder guns and a more extensive support element of mortars and heavy machine guns. It could be argued that it might have been better to send Hicks' brigade into the town rather than the 1st Parachute Brigade; however, Hicks would have to secure a great deal of territory and hold it against attacks from any direction whereas the Parachute Brigade's responsibility really amounted to the Arnhem road bridge and the railway bridge if it could be secured. The other objectives – such as the high ground to the north of the town – could be abandoned if necessary.

Scheduled to arrive at 10am on 18 September, Brigadier Hackett's 4th Parachute Brigade was tasked with relieving the 1st Brigade of responsibility for the north of Arnhem and forming part of an extensive perimeter which would include LZ 'L' as the main supply route for the division until relieved by XXX Corps. Intellectual, versatile and highly experienced, Hackett had grave doubts about the operation as a whole, but not, it would seem, about the role of his brigade. He seems to have been perfectly confident that his three battalions could deal with their tasks so long as everything else went according to plan.

These three brigades formed the normal establishment of the division, however it was obvious that Urquhart's force would be very vulnerable if the Germans were able to organise a concerted attack, especially if XXX Corps did not make rapid progress. A fourth formation was added to the mix; Major General Sosabowski's 1st Polish Parachute Brigade. He, like Hackett, had serious doubts about the viability of Market Garden, but had the utmost confidence in his men. The Polish Brigade, raised from troops who had escaped to Britain in 1940, had been trained at Leven in Scotland and developed many of the techniques practiced by British airborne units. The Poles were to be dropped on the south bank of the river, close to the bridge on the third day of the operation; the very location that the RAF had refused to consider for British paratroops on the first day. The RAF's view was that the anti-aircraft defences around the bridge were formidable, but would have been captured by 1st Parachute Brigade long before the arrival of the Poles. In Sosabowski's view – one borne out by subsequent events – the Market Garden plan simply did not take account of the Germans. The best that he could say – as he confided to Hackett – was that it was a better plan than Comet had been.

Something in the region of 12,000 men were committed to the Arnhem battle. A further 2,200 men and over 1,000 vehicles, the seaborne 'tail' of the division, had arrived on the continent well ahead of the operation and by 17 September were about 12.4 miles (20km) behind the front waiting to rejoin the division when circumstances allowed. Of the airborne element, some would not arrive at all due to enemy action or accidents en route; one of the Polish battalions would eventually be dropped at Grave. The British paratroopers were virtually all volunteers, as were many of the Poles. The Airlanding units – 1st Battalion, the Border Regiment, 7th King's Own Scottish Borderers (KOSBs) and 2nd South Staffordshires had simply been assigned en masse to glider service, rather confirming Field Marshal Slim's opinion that any well-trained battalion could be used in any infantry role.

The British Airborne Soldier

Although the six battalions of the Parachute Regiment assigned to the Airborne Division volunteered for airborne service, the three glider battalions and the divisional troops largely comprised ordinary units that were converted to a glider role, but they all developed a high state of professionalism and élan. Due to the high losses incurred in North Africa and Italy, a very large proportion had never been in action before. Typically, airborne soldiers were a little younger than most troops, but were exceptionally physically fit and had been intensively trained at company and battalion level. With the exception of the chaplains and the medical staff virtually every man in the division could and did take on an infantry role.

The nature of airborne operations excluded any opportunity to introduce the units to the battle by degrees which resulted in some hesitancy in the early stages of the Arnhem action, though this was quickly overcome. A lack of combat experience was probably at the root of a failure to press the early attacks, but the intrinsic quality of the soldier, his training and the leadership made him – as Bittrich said – 'incredible in defence'. All battles are 'soldier's battles' and none more so than Arnhem. Although it is probably true that the Germans could have pressed their attacks more closely at the bridge and the Oosterbeek perimeter and ended the battle more quickly, the cost would have been prohibitive due to the exceptional determination and unshakeable morale of the British troops.

7. British paratroops landing. The angle of view would suggest that the photograph was taken from the air.

Kit

Regardless of the issues surrounding brigade and divisional training, and whether or not they had volunteered to be airborne soldiers, the majority of the men deployed were physically fit and had trained very hard at section, platoon, company and battalion level. Almost all of their armament was identical to that carried by their land-bound comrades, although airborne troops had a distinctive appearance in their famous trademark red berets and Denison Smocks. The beret was worn with pride away from the battlefield, but photographic evidence from Arnhem and Oosterbeek rather suggests that most men chose to wear the airborne steel helmet when in action. This obviously offered better protection against blast and shrapnel and was a less obvious target – partly because it was not red (though Parachute Regiment berets are actually maroon), but also because it was easy to attach foliage to the net supplied to aid camouflage.

THE DENISON SMOCK

The Denison Smock was originally designed as an overall to prevent the parachutist from catching his equipment on struts, boltheads and other obstructions in aircraft, however it proved to be a much more useful piece of equipment and it is clear that paratroops in every theatre retained their smocks as protection against the weather, for the benefit of the camouflage colouring, the extra pockets and, no doubt, simply because of their distinctive appearance. Because the material was dyed, cut out and pieced together randomly, no two smocks are absolutely identical. Although originally intended for the Parachute Regiment battalions, Denison Smocks were widely worn by the Airlanding units as well.

THE LEE–ENFIELD NO. 4 RIFLE

Developed over a period of nearly half a century from a design by Scotsman James Paris Lee (a naturalised American citizen) the No. 4 Mark I rifle was first issued in 1939. The No. 4 Mk I was superseded by the Mk I* in 1942, which was produced by Savage-Stevens Arms in the United States and at the Long Branch Arsenal in Canada.

Accurate and reliable, The No. 4 rifle mounted a spike bayonet and had a 10-round magazine, but many British infantrymen would fill the magazine and then load an eleventh round into the chamber, a practice which was dangerous and put a severe strain on the magazine spring. Little different from earlier models, variants of the No. 4 continued to be the main rifle of the British Army until 1956 and remained in use with other armies for many years thereafter.

The majority carried the Lee–Enfield No. 4 rifle. Adopted in 1928 (though not available in adequate quantities until 1941) it was a very dependable and exceptionally accurate weapon. It was a development of the weapon designed by James Lee and made at Enfield, hence the name. The magazine was designed to hold ten .303 bullets and with steady hands and a good eye it was perfectly possible to hit a man at 500 or even 600 metres, though in practice it was very rare that a soldier would see an enemy at anything more than half that distance. Although it was never adopted for service with the American forces, a great many were made at the Savage factory in the United States and were supplied to Britain through the Lend Lease programme, so a number of them bear the title 'US Property' on the left-hand side of the breech.

The campaign of 1940 had made the British Army aware that there was a pressing need for an equivalent to the German 'Schmeisser' MP40 submachine gun to provide rifle sections with more short-range rapid firepower. This was the origin of the Sten gun, named for its designers Reginald Shepherd and Harold Turpin and the factory where the weapon was developed – Enfield. The Sten's magazine held thirty-two 9mm rounds and had a good rate of fire, but it was cheap and often poorly made. As a result it was unpopular and could be as much a danger to friend as foe; Brigadier Lathbury came very close to accidentally shooting Urquhart in the foot on the first day of the operation. The alternative to the Sten was the American .45 calibre Thompson, which does not seem to have been so widely used on Market Garden as the Sten. Both these weapons fired a 'short' round with less propellant than a rifle bullet and consequently a lower muzzle velocity and range, though neither was very accurate and they were intended for relatively close-quarters action.

More serious firepower was provided by the section machine gun, the Bren. Like the Lee–Enfield rifle it was a .303 calibre weapon. Fed from a 30-round magazine the Bren was air-cooled and was intended to be operated by two men, one to fire the weapon and one to change the magazines and, periodically, the barrel, to prevent overheating. At 20lb (10kg) it was not particularly heavy for a

THE STEN GUN

Conceived as an answer to the German Schmeisser and as a cheaper alternative to the Thompson, the Sten was designed by R. Shepherd and H. Turpin whose surname initials and the first two letters of 'Enfield', home of the Royal Small Arms Factory, produced the name 'Sten'. An unpopular weapon, a Sten was nearly the end of General Urquhart, who narrowly avoided being shot when one was dropped to the floor and promptly discharged several rounds. The Sten went through a process of continuous development throughout the war. Despite its reputation, nearly 4,000,000 were made and because it was so simple to make a German-built version was issued to *Volksturm* (Home Guard) units in early 1945.

machine gun. The Bren's slow rate of fire compared to the German MG34 and MG42, which were generally belt-fed, was not so much of a disadvantage as one might think since it tended to reduce unnecessary expenditure of ammunition.

During his descent, most of the paratrooper's kit was carried in a bag suspended 20ft (6 metres) below him. Inevitably this meant a short delay before the man was ready to fight, but arguably it made the parachute more stable, and since the kit bag would hit ground a second or two before trooper, the chute would billow a little, slowing the man's descent for the last few metres. Some bags broke away from their owners, which was potentially something of a danger to those below, though there is no evidence that many people were hit by free-falling kit bags, however the contents of dropped bags were generally completely ruined.

In addition to the rifles, Stens and Brens of the rifle companies, each battalion carried a number of support weapons, including Vickers machine guns, mortars and PIAT (from the acronym Projector, Infantry, Anti-Tank) anti-tank projectors. The Vickers, like the Bren and the Lee–Enfield, was a .303 calibre weapon, and was a water-cooled, sustained-fire machine gun, issued to the machine gun platoon of each battalion. It was so reliable that it stayed in British Army service until the 1970s. A variant on the Vickers – the Vickers 'K' gun – was originally developed for an anti-aircraft role and for mounting in the turrets of bomber aircraft, but it was also chosen as the main armament of the jeeps used by the Reconnaissance Squadron because of its exceptionally high rate of fire; anything from 850 to 1,200 rounds per minute.

There were two types of mortar available. The 2in. mortar was intended as a platoon-level support weapon. It was fitted with a sight but experienced operators were encouraged to use their own judgement. It could fire a bomb weighing slightly more than 2lb (just over a kilo) to a range of over 400 metres (approx. 200 yards). The 3in. mortar was a battalion-level asset. The mortar platoon comprised eight weapons and provided an integral 'artillery' element, supporting the rifle companies to a range of about a mile.

THE BREN GUN

Essentially a Czech design, developed from the ZB vs 26 Czech light machine gun, the Bren Gun was adopted for the British Army in the 1930s and a small number of the later models were still in use as late as the 1991 Gulf War. According to 1940s British Army myth the weapon was designed by a private soldier named Breen or O' Brien, but in fact the name was constructed from the first two letters of Brno in Czechoslovakia where it was designed and the first two letters of Enfield in England, where it was made. The Bren was exceptionally accurate to about 500 metres. Although the magazine was designed to take thirty .303 bullets, it was preferable to load only twenty-eight to reduce the risk of jamming.

Some of the parachute battalions opted to take only four mortars into battle, replacing them with four Vickers guns. The PIAT was really a grenade launcher. It was quite effective at close range and unlike the American Bazooka or German Panzerfaust, which were essentially rocket launchers, there was no back-blast so the PIAT was easier and safer when firing from confined spaces. However, it could be dangerous to the operator. Captain Cain, who had become something of an anti-tank specialist and had fired about fifty bombs during the operation, was injured when a '… bomb went off in the Piat. I got bits of stuff in my face and two black eyes. It blew me over backwards and I was blind'. Fortunately for the captain his blindness was temporary. He was soon back in the fight and would go on to win one of the five Victoria Crosses awarded for actions during the Arnhem battle.

The only other infantry weapons that could be deployed against armoured vehicles were the standard hand grenade – crucial for the close fighting – and the Gammon bomb. Officially known as the

No. 82 grenade, the Gammon bomb was named for its designer, Captain R.S. Gammon of 1st Parachute Regiment and was basically a form of satchel charge, intended primarily for demolition purposes.

Two anti-tank guns were issued to airborne units; the 6 pounder and the 17 pounder. The more common 6 pounder was adequate against armoured cars and half tracks and some of the earlier model German tanks and self-propelled guns, but the crews found it almost impossible to penetrate the armour of the more advanced tanks – the Panther and Tiger. Nearly sixty 6 pounders were taken to Arnhem. The 17 pounder was – as the name suggests – a much heavier weapon and was used by two troops of each of the Airlanding batteries; giving a total of sixteen guns. It was certainly very effective, but there were not enough of them to meet the demands of the situation. It was possible to tow a 17 pounder with a Bren Carrier, but it was really too heavy and a number of Morris tractors were adapted for delivery by the Hamilcar glider. The use of anti-tank guns seems to have been something of a weakness among the parachute battalions. The gunners could not hunt down the tank; rather the tank had to be drawn to a position where they could engage it. A number of guns were lost through a failure to give them proper protection and this may have stemmed from the fact that the parachute battalions, unlike the Airlanding units, did not have their own integral anti-tank platoons.

The Bren or 'Universal' Carrier was a lightly armoured tracked vehicle, designed for the transport of rapid close support in line with infantry battalions and widely used to tow the 6 pounder gun, though airborne units often used the ubiquitous jeep instead. Indeed, airborne units viewed the carrier as more of a transport item for the delivery of ammunition in combat. It had a vast range of applications – casualty evacuation, reconnaissance, transporting Observation Post staff and the collection and distribution of supplies by the Royal Army Service Corps (RASC). Each parachute battalion's mortar platoon had two glider-borne carriers to transport ammunition, but it would seem that at least one unit –

8. A Bren Carrier being unloaded from a Hamilcar glider.

2nd Battalion – was obliged at the last minute to leave one of their carriers behind due to aircraft shortage, dramatically reducing the amount of ammunition available for the battle. Each mortar team consisted of three men to carry the weapon itself (dismantled into the tube, the base-plate and the bipod) with the other members of the platoon each carrying six of the 10lb (nearly 5kg) bombs. This was a heavy burden for the men, but only represented a few minutes of firing, so the loss of one carrier had serious consequences in terms of ammunition supply.

The artillery element of the division consisted of two batteries of anti-tank guns and three of light field pieces. The latter were each equipped with six 75mm Pack Howitzers, which were effective weapons and well suited to the needs of the airborne force. The Pack Howitzer had a shorter range and lighter shell than the

THE BREN CARRIER

The carrier had no real equivalent outside the British and Commonwealth armies and was originally issued to serve as a mobile platform for infantry support weapons – primarily machine guns and mortars. With a total production run of well over 100,000 vehicles from 1934 to 1960 the carrier is far and away the most extensively produced armoured fighting vehicle in history. Used for any number of tasks from gun tractor to casualty evacuation and general battlefield transport, carriers were issued to parachute battalions to transport mortar platoons and to carry ammunition. Weighing nearly 4 tons, carriers were transported by glider. Considerable numbers were captured by the Germans and by the Japanese who – like the British – put them to a wide variety of uses.

25 pounder gun which was the backbone of the field artillery in other divisions, but was light enough for the gliders and could be towed by a jeep.

The majority of the equipment issued to the Airborne Division was of a decent quality and performed well, but one crucial exception was communication devices. At divisional, brigade and battalion level the various radio sets proved unreliable and inadequate, in part due to the high concentration of metals in the soil, which interfered with the signals. The officer who formed the Signals Regiment for 1st Airborne Division in 1942, Richard Moberley, wrote about this to author Christopher Hibbert in about 1961, telling him that the '22' set had been selected before it came into production and although it had been '… fairly successful in North Africa, Italy and Normandy. It turned out quite unsuitable for Arnhem'. He went on to say that the War Office had refused to countenance demands for better equipment and that 'the position was made worse by the reluctance of commanders to allot additional airlift for bulky wireless sets as this would have meant

75mm Pack Howitzer

The weapon was designed for the United States Army in the 1920s and 1930s to provide a light and easily movable artillery piece for operations in challenging terrain. Constructed in such a way that it could be broken down into elements light enough to be transported by pack animals, it was the obvious choice for the two Airlanding regiments raised to support airborne operations, though in fact a total of more than 800 were supplied to British forces in the war years. Pack 75s remained in British service until the 1950s.

9. 75mm Pack Howitzer of the 1st Light Regiment in action.

fewer fighting men'. Major Deane Drummond, second-in-command of the divisional signals unit at Arnhem, made a similar point to historian Martin Middlebrook; that the division covered too large an area for the equipment assigned to parachute formations, although a greater number of the more powerful '19' sets would have required '… more jeeps and more gliders, but any change in allocation would have implications for other units'. One success in communications was the homing system used by the Independent Company to guide in the main drops on 11 and 18 September. The system comprised two separate units, a 'Eureka' transmitter on the ground, and 'Rebecca' receivers fitted to the aircraft.

Obviously every piece of equipment that was too heavy or too delicate to be dropped by parachute had to travel by glider and two models were used at Arnhem: the Horsa and the Hamilcar. Both aircraft were reliable and surprisingly sturdy, but they each had drawbacks. The Horsas were difficult to load and heavier equipment could only be unloaded by removing the tail assembly. In theory this was effected by the removal of a number of 'quick-release' bolts, but these could easily be damaged on landing and were not very reliable if the glider came to rest in anything other than an even keel, so extricating the contents of the glider could be a time-consuming practice and obviously a dangerous undertaking if the landing zone was under fire. It took fifty-two Horsas to transport one battalion and the shortage of tugs and gliders meant that half of one unit, the South Staffordshires, was delayed until

THE HORSA GLIDER

Over 3,700 Airspeed Horsas were built between 1941 and 1945. It could carry up to twenty-nine infantrymen, was normally towed at about 75mph (120km/hour) and was the workhorse of all major British glider operations. In addition to carrying the three infantry battalions of 1st Airlanding Brigade, Horsas carried jeeps, anti-tank weapons, divisional troops and medical staff to the battle. The majority of the 1,200 Horsas committed to the Arnhem operation were flown by officers and sergeants of the Glider Pilot Regiment. Four hundred Horsas were used by United States forces and ten non-flying replicas were constructed for use in the 1977 film *A Bridge Too Far*.

10. Airspeed Horsa – Horsa gliders; two have been split in the centre in order to remove jeeps or 6 pounder anti-tank guns.

the second lift, thus reducing the infantry complement that the Airlanding Brigade needed to carry out their task of protecting the drop and landing zones.

The cockpit of the much larger Hamilcar sat on top of the aircraft and the entire nose cone could be lifted up to allow jeeps and carriers to be driven straight out of the fuselage, but the raised cockpit put the pilots at great risk if the glider should turn over on landing.

Almost all of the paratroopers were dropped from Dakota aircraft, which were also used as glider tugs, along with Albemarle and Stirling bombers. Urquhart's staff estimated that they required about 130 Dakotas for each of the parachute brigades. In all, more than 500 transport aircraft and over 350 gliders were committed to the first day of the operation, accompanied by a huge force of fighters to protect against German intervention.

I I. LZ 'Z' with a mixture of Horsa and Hamilcar gliders. The Hamilcars were used to deliver 17 pounder anti-tank guns, Morris gun tractors and Bren Carriers as they were too large and too heavy for the Horsa gliders.

Aircraft losses on the first lift were relatively low, but increased dramatically thereafter. As long as the Germans maintained contact with their garrisons in the channel ports they could rely on an hour's warning of the arrival of each convoy of aircraft and could therefore alert both their fighter squadrons and their anti-aircraft units in good time.

The ground element of Market Garden – the three corps of Second Army – was largely equipped along the same lines as the parachute and airborne battalions. The men of the infantry battalions carried the same Lee–Enfield rifle, Sten and Bren guns and used the same anti-tank weapons, and platoon and battalion mortars. These battalions were to operate in concert with armoured regiments, most of which used the American-built Sherman or British Churchill tank. The Churchill was mechanically sound and quite well armoured, but slow and seriously under-gunned, however it did provide

THE DOUGLAS C47

More widely known as the 'Dakota', the C47 first flew
in December 1941. It had a wingspan of 29 metres and
a range of over 994 miles (1,600km), cruising at 149mph
(240km/hour), reduced to around 75mph (120km/hour)
when towing a glider. The reliability and payload capacity
of the Dakota made it a popular aircraft and they were
used extensively in all of the major fronts by USAAF
and RAF squadrons. Over 1,300 Dakotas were used to
drop paratroops and tow gliders for the Market Garden
operation and its remarkable airworthiness means that a
considerable number are still flying today.

12. Men of 1st Battalion the Parachute Regiment in a C47 Dakota en route to Arnhem.

13. A British Sherman at Nijmegen. Although mechanically reliable, the Sherman was no match for the German Panther and Tiger tanks.

an excellent basis for any number of specialist adaptations from flamethrowers to bridge-layers. The Sherman – the workhorse of the Allied armies from 1942 to 1945 – was built in huge numbers, something like 40,000 by the end of the war. The Sherman was reasonably fast and very reliable, but also under-gunned and under-armoured compared to its German counterparts. It was particularly prone to catching fire, which gave rise to two macabre nicknames: 'Tommy Cookers' and 'Ronsons' – a play on a cigarette lighter advert of the day because 'Ronsons light first time'. A wide variety of other armoured vehicles could be found in XXX Corps, including light 'Stuart' tanks, which though outdated, were fast and still in use for reconnaissance purposes, along with Dingo, Humber and Daimler armoured cars and the ubiquitous M3 Half-track which was used to ferry infantry across the battlefield, pick up casualties and could be fitted with anti-aircraft weapons or 75mm guns to provide close support for the infantry.

The Germans

The standard German rifle, the Kar 98 was less accurate and less reliable than the Lee–Enfield and had a smaller magazine, but the rest of the German small arms were of high quality. The Schmeisser submachine gun and the MG34 and MG42 'Spandau' machine guns were reliable and accurate, and the MG42 had a high rate of fire, equalled only by the Vickers 'K' gun. This was a mixed blessing since ammunition was consumed at a prodigious rate and it became common practice for every soldier in a squad to have to carry a belt of ammunition. Despite this, the MG42 has influenced machine gun design ever since its introduction in 1942.

Germany produced a very wide range of armoured fighting vehicles throughout the war, which gave them a technological edge over the Allies, but also meant that it was impossible to produce adequate quantities of any one model. Additionally, each generation of tank was rushed into production without enough time to deal with design problems and a lack of mechanical reliability was a serious issue. The famous Tiger and Panther tanks saw action at Arnhem and against the advance of XXX Corps, but most of the tanks deployed against the Airborne Division were Mark III and Mark IV Panzers. A number of French Renaults captured from the French in 1940 and retained for training purposes were thrown into the battle but proved to be no match for the 6 pounder guns and PIATs of the Airlanding Brigade, and they were all lost very quickly.

Lighter armoured vehicles were used in greater numbers than tanks in the battle, partly because there were more available and partly because armoured cars are more manoeuvrable. The Germans also employed considerable numbers of Sturmgeschutz or 'Stug' assault guns mounted on enclosed, tracked armoured vehicles, differing from tanks in that they did not have a rotating turret and thus the whole vehicle had to be turned and pointed towards the enemy. Although less versatile than a tank, the Stug was very much cheaper to produce and was used to provide mobile

STURMGESCHUTZ ASSAULT GUN

Designed to provide mobile close-support artillery for the infantry, this series of vehicles – often called 'Stugs' – were built in very large quantities and were deployed to every front. A great many were built on the same basic chassis of the Panzerkampfwagen III tank, and in fact 'Stug IIIs' were produced in greater quantities than any other German combat vehicle of the war. The fixed superstructure was very much cheaper to build than the rotating turret of a conventional tank, but could render the vehicle vulnerable and a considerable number were destroyed during the Arnhem battle.

close support to infantry units. It had no direct equivalent in either the British or American armies and was more vulnerable than a conventional tank in armoured combat, but it was a powerful tool against the lightly armed airborne troops at Arnhem.

The German approach to training gave them a huge organisational advantage throughout the war and this was particularly important in the Arnhem battle. Relatively junior officers and even NCOs were encouraged to act on their own initiative to a much greater degree and the rank and file were much more carefully prepared for the experience of serving together in ad hoc combat groups assembled from disparate bodies of men serving under officers and NCOs that they did not know. Although men tended to stay in one unit, the 'family' tradition of British infantry regiments was not such a major factor in German formations. This was reflected at all levels and German commanders were much more at ease with combining units from different divisions to carry out specific tasks or to react to developments than their British counterparts. There were, from time to time, chain of command issues arising from combining Wehrmacht and SS troops into ad hoc formations, but as a rule, it was generally accepted and understood that the exigencies

Wilhelm Bittrich

Born on 26 February 1894, Wilhelm Bittrich served as a fighter pilot in the First World War. After the war he joined the 'Freikorps' movement during the troubled years of the Weimar Republic. Although he had no regard for the main political figures of the Nazi party, he was in sympathy with many of their ideals, primarily the reconstruction of a strong and independent Germany. He joined the SS Division Leibstandarte Adolf Hitler in 1939 and commanded the 'Deutschland' Regiment in Poland later that year and in France during 1940. He moved on to command 2nd SS Panzer Division for a spell before taking command of II SS Panzer Corps, which consisted of 9th 'Hohenstaufen' and 10th 'Frundsberg' divisions and was thus the senior German battlefield commander at Arnhem.

Bittrich was a very talented general with high professional and ethical standards. Albert Speer visited him immediately after the Arnhem battle and found the general:

> ... in a state of fury. The day before, his Second Tank Corps had virtually wiped out a British airborne division. During the fighting the general had made an arrangement permitting the enemy to run a field hospital behind the German lines. But party functionaries had taken it upon themselves to kill captured British and American pilots, and Bittrich looked like a liar.
>
> William Buckingham, *Arnhem*

Bittrich served as a corps commander in Austria during the Vienna Offensive of 2–13 April, but abandoned Vienna rather than see his troops or the city destroyed. He took no part in public life after the war and died in hospital in 1979.

14. Bittrich. (Bundesarchiv, Bild 146-1971-033-49 / CC-BY-SA)

The German Soldier

Far from consisting of 'old men and boys' the German force available at Arnhem proved to be a formidable opponent. The enormous variety of German troops deployed to Arnhem makes it impossible to define a 'typical' German soldier. At one end of the spectrum there was 9th SS Panzer Division; badly battered from the campaign through France and woefully short of men and armoured vehicles, but well led, extremely experienced and highly motivated. Aware that the battle was there to be won, they proved to be an effective and determined enemy.

At the opposite extreme the German forces included large numbers of sailors with no ships and airmen with no planes who were thrown into the battle with little or no infantry training as well as a substantial number of Dutch and other 'non-German' troops who must have been very aware that the war was already lost and whose futures were correspondingly bleak.

Although the strategic outlook was bad, the tactical situation was more promising. The Market Garden operation was extremely ambitious and from the second day of the battle it was clear that the position of the Airborne Division was precarious. The Germans enjoyed a number of advantages; their lines of communication were secure and they were not impeded by shortages of ammunition or food. The senior officers were versatile, skilful and experienced leaders who enjoyed the confidence of the troops and who were not afraid to use their initiative.

15. German infantry moving along a ditch in the Arnhem area. (Bundesarchiv, Bild 183-S73822 / CC-BY-SA)

of combat situations might demand radical reorganisation and that the formalities of the normal command structure could be ignored depending on the tactical circumstances.

The Germans were also rather more innovative. In the later years of the war, the Germans often suffered from a lack of light armour, but were prepared to use assets in very different roles to the ones for which they had been designed. Assigning mobile anti-aircraft guns, particularly multi-barrelled automatic weapons to an infantry support role is a case in point and many such vehicles were deployed at Arnhem.

The Strategy

The Market Garden plan was simple in principle; to mount one massive thrust which would provide an avenue to push Montgomery's Second Army over the Rhine and on into Germany. Eisenhower felt that a broader advance, involving all of the Allied army groups, was a better policy, but he had some sympathy with Montgomery and was willing to give him a degree of preferential treatment in the allocation of supplies. This was not enough for Montgomery, who felt that his plan should be given absolute priority even at the expense of bringing the operations of Patton and Devers to a complete halt. In practice, increasing the supply allocation to Second Army was one thing; ensuring the timely arrival of that material was another. Almost everything had to come by truck from Normandy and the situation could not be improved unless the Allies captured one or more ports closer to the front. Montgomery's preference for a single thrust was a questionable policy. As Eisenhower pointed out, such a thrust would produce a huge salient with immensely long and vulnerable flanks which, as it progressed, would require several divisions to ensure secure supply until eventually there would be no force left at the front. It was a risky proposition, and potentially disastrous; if it failed to break the German Army, then they might be able to mount a counter-offensive, cut across the base of the salient and force the surrender of a major force which could not be replaced, especially given Allied commitments in Italy and the Far East. Additionally, if the Allies were held at the Rhine, the Russians might well be able to conquer the whole of Germany which would have implications for the post-war settlement. On the other hand, forcing a passage through the Netherlands and across the Rhine might well break the back of German resistance.

Montgomery persuaded Eisenhower that the potential benefits outweighed the risks and proceeded with the plan on the basis that Market Garden would have absolute priority over all other operations. This was not quite what had actually been agreed. Eisenhower was very clear that operations elsewhere had to be maintained to prevent the Germans from regrouping in front of Patton and Devers and of course to prevent them concentrating their efforts in front of Second Army. Further, the description of Eisenhower's preference for a 'broad front' as described by Montgomery in his memoirs is somewhat misleading. Eisenhower did not envisage a front that stretched right across Europe from north to south, but rather simultaneous advances – Montgomery in the north, Bradley in the centre and the American Seventh Army from the south. His intention was to divide German strength and also to allow the rapid exploitation of one or other axis of advance as the situation developed.

Montgomery's preference for what he called a single 'full-blooded thrust' was acceptable to Eisenhower as a step on the road toward victory, but it was not likely to result in an immediate and total collapse of German resistance. Eisenhower did not accept that Market Garden would bring about an opportunity to make a dash across Germany all the way to Berlin. Montgomery probably did not think so either, but it is possible that he hoped to establish Second Army's advance as the real focus of the campaign in Europe by bringing about a situation that would demand Eisenhower's unstinting support and, effectively, restore Montgomery's position as the principal battlefield commander in the war against Germany; a position he had enjoyed until Eisenhower assumed the role of supreme commander from 1 September 1944. He had competition in the shape of General Patton, who, with the tacit cooperation of General Bradley, constantly re-interpreted his orders to achieve the same goal. When authorised to make reconnaissance operations, Patton made them in such strength that they became battles from which he could not withdraw without serious risks.

Montgomery was dismissive of the efforts of others and, among British historians at least, has benefitted from a rather uncritical acceptance of his ability. He was not always successful, and when he was, his operations had always been planned in great detail over a long period, with stores assembled in vast quantities and with formations and units which had been intensively trained for the operation in hand. Interestingly, Montgomery had remarkably little to say about Market Garden in his memoirs.

He was undoubtedly a difficult colleague – perhaps because he did not see himself in a collegiate situation. He was prone to viewing any deviation from a plan forced by enemy action or mistakes as having actually been part of the plan in the first place, thus enhancing his reputation and building an uncritical acceptance that if Montgomery said a thing could be done then it could be done. Even so, his implied belief that the Germans were about to crack and that the war could be ended before Christmas was not universally accepted. Churchill believed that if Germany collapsed before the end of 1944 the reasons would be 'political rather than purely military'. He had a good point. Germany still had nearly 3,500,000 men under arms and would be able to mobilise more in *Volksturm* (Home Guard) formations once the war crossed the Rhine. A political collapse was not too likely either. The failure of the Stauffenberg plot to assassinate Hitler and the reprisals thereafter discouraged overt opposition to the Nazi regime. The German generals were also unlikely to express dissent for fear of the firing squad – or worse – and the political leadership was not only secure, but had nothing to gain by ending the war quickly on the only terms the Allies would accept – unconditional surrender. The romantic notion cherished by some German leaders of coming to terms with the Western Allies and continuing the war against Russia was never remotely realistic. Even if it had been acceptable to Western leaders – which it was not – it would not have been acceptable to public opinion in Britain, America or France. This was a matter of some consequence. The French leadership was eager to see Germany defeated and by late 1944, a French Army of some stature was fast becoming a reality as the pre-war army was reconstituted with British and American equipment. This new army made a relatively modest contribution to the war effort, but would certainly be required as an occupation force in Germany when the war was over, so French political opinion could not be ignored.

THE DAYS BEFORE BATTLE

The crossing of the Seine and the fall of Paris had been landmarks on the road to Berlin, but forcing a crossing of the Rhine would present more of a challenge for several reasons. As the last geographical obstacle protecting the Reich, the Rhine held a very real significance for the Germans. If the Allies could be stopped in the west there was a possibility – however slim – that the course of the war in the east could be turned in Germany's favour. From a post-war perspective this seems to be an impossible proposition, but the picture looked very different to a lot of Germans in 1944. There were certainly many German officers who believed that the Reich was finished, but there were others who hoped for a brighter future. Field Marshal Model, Commander-in-Chief of Army Group B, specifically forbade his subordinates from demolishing the Rhine bridges at Nijmegen and Arnhem because he intended to use them in a counterattack that would drive the Allies back through Belgium, forcing them to regroup.

One might question where the resources were to come from for such operations, but it is worth remembering that the Germans did in fact mount a major offensive in the winter of 1944 which posed a serious threat to Allied plans. The river barriers that presented an obstacle to the advancing Allies represented an opportunity for the Germans. Clearly any barrier to the Allies was also a bulwark

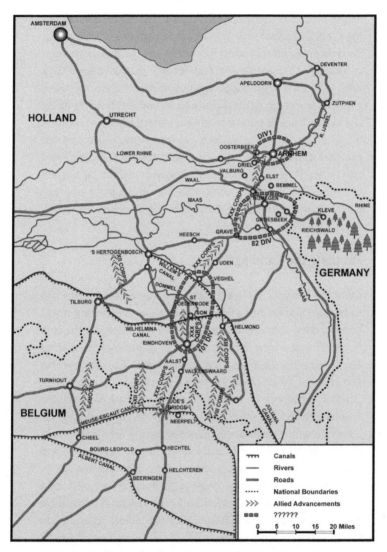

16. The Market Garden plan, September 1944. (Courtesy of Lloyd Clark, Arnhem)

behind which the Germans could regroup their battered forces, but the rivers also provided an opportunity to gather in units that had become detached from their formations and the thousands upon thousands of individuals who had become separated from their units. Each of the target bridges was potentially a 'choke point' where a handful of men could prevent troops and vehicles from retreating any further. Many of these troops were perfectly willing to continue the fight; they had just lost contact with the command structure that could tell them where to deploy. The rest – however unwilling – had little choice. They could either do as they were told and be assigned to existing – if depleted – units or to ad hoc groups, or else they could explain their refusal to Wehrmacht and SS military policemen.

Planning the Landings

Once the principle of Market Garden was accepted, the idea had to be consolidated into a practical plan. General Browning would command the airborne element and General Horrocks the land forces. In appearance, Browning was the epitome of the dashing British officer; always immaculately dressed and full of vigour, he had proven to be gallant officer in the First World War, but had no real practical experience as a battlefield commander. He had been the ideal choice to form the airborne forces when the need was for someone with extensive experience in dealing with government departments and the army establishment. Initially his function, and that of his headquarters staff, had been purely administrative, but by the summer of 1944 he was eager to get into the fight. He took a leading role in developing Market Garden, which was understandable but unwise. He seems to have had little grasp of the practical aspects of the battle. Two glaring examples of this were his instructions regarding Nijmegen and his decision to take his own headquarters to the battle. General Gavin's 82nd Division was given responsibility for the sector south of Nijmegen, but Browning expressly ordered him to concentrate his efforts at Nijmegen to securing and holding

17. Field Marshal Montgomery and Lieutenant General Horrocks. (Courtesy of Tim Lynch)

the Groesbeek Heights to prevent the Germans using it as an assembly area for attacks on the corridor that XXX Corps would pass through en route to Arnhem. Gavin was specifically ordered not to make any attempt on the Nijmegen Bridge itself, but to leave that to XXX Corps. This imperilled the whole operation. Had the Germans demolished the Nijmegen Bridge – and General Heinz Harmel had ordered charges to be laid for that very purpose – there would have been no value whatsoever in the 1st Airborne Division securing the bridge at Arnhem and victory would have been handed to the Germans on a plate. In fact Gavin wisely did everything he could to arrange an attempt on the bridge behind Browning's back, but the size of his force and the extent of his responsibilities within the Market Garden plan made this impossible.

Browning's decision to take his Airborne Corps headquarters (HQ) to the battlefield simply defies comprehension on any practical level and seems to have been driven by his desire to be seen as taking an active part in what was hoped and expected to be a major strategic victory. The airborne element of Market Garden would inevitably be a matter of three distinct divisional battles; there was neither opportunity or necessity to coordinate the efforts of the divisions, so there was really nothing for the corps headquarters to do and even if there had been, Browning's HQ was an administrative organisation; it simply was not designed to fulfil tactical responsibilities. To make matters worse, Browning's staff would require more than thirty gliders which would otherwise have been available for the British airlift to Arnhem. Consequently, Urquhart would have half a battalion less to commit to the first day of the battle.

Most importantly, Browning failed to persuade the RAF to deliver the airborne troops to where they needed to be at the right time or in the numbers required for the job. Alternative dropping and landing zones had been considered. Open ground immediately to the south of Arnhem Bridge was rejected by British intelligence as being reclaimed 'Polder' and too soft for the safe landing of gliders; a view supported by the Dutch officers familiar with the terrain. The area was intersected by a large number of deep drainage ditches which could cause gliders to tumble upside down on landing and there was also the question of aircraft overshooting their target and dropping the troops into the fast-flowing river or among the buildings on the north bank, which would be likely to result in unacceptable casualties during the drop. Several officers, including Frost, seem to have been of the opinion that it would be worth accepting heavier casualties on the drop zone for the sake of being delivered to the objective rather than at a distance of half a day's march. A further barrier to the use of this area was the concentration of flak installations around the bridge itself. The perceived risk was sufficient to be used as a major argument against deploying a portion of 1st Parachute Brigade to this zone on the first day of the operation, though was believed that the guns would be neutralised by the third day when the Polish Brigade would be dropped there to reinforce 1st Airborne. Since the glider element of the Polish Brigade would be arriving on Monday 18 September as part of the second lift there would be no danger to the transport aircraft, though the risk of Polish paratroops drowning in the river seems to have been ignored.

An area of open heath to the north of the city was another possibility, but it was not believed to be extensive enough for glider landings. It would, perhaps, have been adequate for parachute units and it could be argued that landing one or more of 1st Parachute Brigade's battalions there would have allowed troops to enter the town much more quickly, however not all of the elements of the brigade would actually drop from aircraft. The anti-tank, field

FLAK

Mobile anti-aircraft guns on trucks or half-tracks were used extensively by the Germans as surface weapons throughout the war to offset shortages of tanks and armoured reconnaissance vehicles. Considerable numbers of mobile anti-aircraft weapons were deployed at Arnhem, partly due to the absence of other combat vehicles and partly because there were a good number available, but also because of the high rate of fire that could be applied – particularly from multi-barrelled weapons – and the good manoeuvrability of trucks and half-tracks in built-up areas.

18. 101st Airborne inspecting a broken glider in Holland.

ambulance, engineers and ammunition vital to a successful operation would all require gliders. There again, just one battalion landing north of the city would have given the Germans a more complex challenge to deal with; there would have been troops behind the stop-line which the Germans so quickly put in place. The final selection, some 6.2 miles (10km) or more from the objective was chosen by the RAF, largely on the basis of the flak risk from around Arnhem and from Deelen airfield to the north of Arnhem. Convoys of aircraft would have just enough room to drop paratroops and deliver gliders before turning for home.

The staged delivery of 1st Airborne Division to its target area does not seem to have been of great concern to anyone other than Urquhart and his brigade commanders, yet was surely one of the major problems of the operation. Yet again, the presence and activity of the German Army seems to have been conveniently kicked into the long grass. If the objective was glaringly obvious from the moment the landings started, it is incomprehensible that no one, with the exception of General Sosabowski, gave any real thought to how the German command would react and what resources they might be able to bring to bear in the two days that the scheduling allowed for the arrival of XXX Corps, let alone allowing for the thought that the leading elements of Horrocks' force might not arrive in that time.

Although it would have been a challenge, it would have been possible to land the airborne forces at dawn, return to Britain, embark a second lift and be back over the battle area by the middle of the afternoon. The three airborne divisional commanders – Urquhart, Taylor and Gavin – would have had all or most of their assets in action by dusk and the Germans would have had less opportunity to disrupt the airlifts of the second day. This would have had the greatest effect on the British division. Not only would the infantry force have been nearly twice as strong, fewer men would have been needed to retain drop zones for the next day. Weather conditions would have been less of an issue; as it turned out the second Market Garden lift was delayed for several hours due to fog in England. Finally, with all of 1st Airborne on the ground on 17 September, Urquhart's force could have been reinforced by the Polish Brigade on the 18th, when there was still some hope of success.

The plan was questionable, but the failure to act on intelligence is incomprehensible. Major Brian Urquhart (no relation to General Urquhart) had learned from 21st Army intelligence that two German formations – probably 9th and 10th SS Panzer were assembling in the Arnhem area. Concerned about the operation in general and local German activity in particular, Urquhart arranged for a reconnaissance Spitfire to make a pass over the operational area. The Spitfire procured photographs of Mk III and Mk IV tanks around town. Urquhart immediately took these to Browning, who dismissed the evidence, suggesting that the tanks were few in number and that they were probably not fully operational. Browning arranged a meeting between Urquhart and Brigadier Eaggers, the senior medical officer of the Airborne Corps. Eaggers believed that

19. General Sosabowski of the Polish Parachute Brigade talking with General Browning. After the battle Browning, Horrocks and Thomas would shamelessly endeavour to shift the blame for the failure of the operation onto Sosabowski.

the major was absolutely right to be concerned, but, under orders from Browning, Eaggers arranged to have Urquhart sent home on sick leave.

There is an argument that the operation was already too far advanced for cancellation, that everything was prepared and everyone ready to go. This is not convincing. All that was required to put a stop to the airborne element was to order the units not to embark on their aircraft. As for the ground offensive, XXX Corps did not start its advance until the air armada was actually over the heads of the forward units.

Whether Browning really believed in the operation at all is open to question. He is famously credited with telling Montgomery that although he had confidence in the operation, he felt they might be going 'a bridge too far'. It is not clear that he actually said anything of the kind, save in a conversation with Urquhart immediately after the battle. There is a scent of wisdom after the event, but more importantly, if true, this strongly suggests that Browning did not really understand the strategic value of the operation at all. Without the final bridge in the chain – Arnhem – the others had no real value and several divisions would have been committed to a hard fight with no useful outcome.

To compound matters, the Market Garden plan did not really take adequate account of the situation of Horrocks' XXX Corps. The supply effort was already precarious and was unlikely to improve as long as there was massive congestion in the rear of Second Army and both the units and the commanders were reaching the limits of their endurance. Neither the congestion nor the immediate tactical situation was likely to improve. XXX Corps would have to fight its way along one narrow road and even very light enemy forces, if determined, would be able to impose considerable delays.

Intelligence staff considered that enemy assets in the Arnhem area amounted to something like six infantry battalions (perhaps a 'bayonet strength' of 2,500 men at most) with about twenty-five guns and twenty tanks to support them. Reports from Dutch underground sources indicated the presence of armoured units a few miles to the west, but that these units were very much below strength. This was true; the formations in question had taken a terrible beating in France and were in the process of refitting, but they were far from incapable. Moreover, the German Army was generally suffering from a shortage of manpower, but it was still a formidable organisation and the air forces of Britain and America could not hope to completely prevent the Germans moving units into the Arnhem area. Furthermore, although 1st Airborne Division would be strengthened by the Polish Brigade, it would be a full three days before the entire force was on the ground and that was assuming that there would be no delays imposed by bad weather; rather an optimistic assumption.

Optimism was, however, the order of the day. An intelligence summary for 21st Army Group (the parent formation of Second Army) dated 12 September referred to 'several hundred thousand [German] soldiers' and 'superfluous headquarters' making their way eastwards with 'no firm destinations and no firm orders'. It does not seem to have occurred to anyone that these soldiers – or at least a proportion of them – might yet be rallied, assigned to the 'superfluous headquarters' and be sent back into the battle.

As though these issues were not enough, the 'wishful thinking' that characterises so much of the Market Garden operation seems to have pervaded every aspect of the planning process. The capacity of the Luftwaffe was underestimated. The first lift was not seriously troubled, but subsequent lifts came under considerable attack. The Luftwaffe was eventually able to amass about 300 aircraft for operations in the Market Garden area. In general terms the RAF fighter strength operating on the northern axis of the Allied advance was technically and numerically capable of dealing with a German effort on that scale, but again that was dependent on favourable weather conditions. It seems to have escaped everyone's notice that autumn fogs are not uncommon in the regions of France and Belgium where the fighters were based. Like the ground element the planners had not given much thought to the Germans, only to the practicalities of mounting the operation.

The XXX Corps' Plan

The XXX Corps' plan was that the attack would be led by Guards Armoured Division with the Irish Guard's battle group advancing from Neerpelt to Eindhoven and Nijmegen and on to Arnhem. It would then be replaced by 43rd (Wessex) Division, which would expand the bridgehead to Apeldoorn, taking Deelen airfield to facilitate the delivery of the Scottish 52nd Lowland Division to the battlefield.

The XXX Corps' reserve would be 50th (Northumberland) Division. The 43rd Division was to be supplied with vast quantities of bridging material, allowing for the possibility that any of the crucial river crossings might be destroyed, though little thought

20. Tanks of XXX Corps en route to Arnhem passing crowds of enthusiastic Netherlanders.

seems to have been given to the length of time it would take to erect such a bridge.

A major flaw with XXX Corps' plan was that there was clearly no intention of mounting the attack at an appropriately early hour. There is no satisfactory explanation for this. It has been suggested that Horrocks was not included in the planning process and was not made aware of the operation until the day before the attack. Clearly this is not the case; in fact he had received his instructions from Montgomery on 12 September. On the 16th he briefed his senior officers, famously telling them that 'this is a tale you will tell your grandchildren ... and mightily bored they'll be'. By the

TARTAN

Captain James Ogilvie of the Glider Pilot Regiment and at least one other officer defied standing orders and wore kilts into battle at Arnhem. The kilt had been abandoned on War Office instructions in 1940, but the appearance of many kilted Scottish soldiers in newsreel films and photographs of the period clearly indicate that they were prepared to ignore the order given the opportunity.

morning of the 17th he was at an advanced observation post waiting for the operation to start and did not give the order for the Guards to start their advance until airborne forces were in sight. He may have felt that the combination of a massive air fleet overhead, a heavy bombardment and the attack by the Irish Guards would cause a collapse of German defences, but this is far from convincing. The airborne forces were not actually dropping right on top of the German troops opposing the Guards Armoured Division, so as far as those men were concerned the airborne force could have been going anywhere, and it is quite likely that many of them just assumed that a massive daylight bombing raid was in progress. Alternatively, Horrocks may have felt that an earlier advance might have warned the Germans that a major operation was under way – which it was. The Germans, however, had been fighting XXX Corps for some time along the same axis and can have been in no doubt that crossing the Rhine was the general British objective, so there was no reason that an early morning advance would have made them think that an airborne assault was imminent.

In fact, the Irish Guards did not start their advance until two hours after the airborne descent started. The first moves on the ground were tactically inept – unusual for Horrocks, who was a competent and conscientious officer with a good track record. Failure to advance at or shortly after dawn meant the loss of the major part of a day when time was clearly of the essence; the timetable for the whole operation was already very tight if XXX Corps were to relieve Airborne in two days.

Alternatively, Horrocks may have had doubts about the operation going ahead at all. Plenty of previous airborne operations had been cancelled in the preceding months, although mostly because the advance of ground troops had been so rapid that targets envisaged had been overrun, but a rapid movement of the frontline had not been the case in September. Overall, there seems to have been no good reason to hold back from attacking early on the 17th, but there were many good reasons to start rolling as early as possible. Apart from the tight schedule, important as that was, the attack would focus German attention on Neerpelt and, if made with sufficient strength and vigour, would be likely to draw units there from neighbouring areas. In any case, since an attack was being made, the longer the delay, the longer the Germans would have to improve defences, expedite their ongoing re-organisation and distribute supplies to their forward units. Although Market Garden achieved complete surprise, the Germans organised their response with commendable speed and efficiency despite many of the troops having lost virtually everything in the retreat from Normandy:

Now we immediately received weapons. Everyone got a rifle and 90 rounds of ammunition which was stuffed into our pockets or haversacks because we no longer had our ammunition pouches, steel helmets or entrenching tools.

Corporal Paul Mueller, from R. Kershaw,
It Never Snows in September

The Landings Commence

> Wherever I looked I could see aircraft, troop transports and large
> aircraft towing gliders. They flew both in formation and singly. It
> was an immense stream which passed quite low over the house.
> I was greatly impressed by the spectacle and I must confess that
> during these minutes the danger of the situation never occurred
> to me. I merely recalled with some regret my own earlier airborne
> operations and when my chief of staff joined me on the balcony I
> could only remark 'Oh how I wish that I ever had such a powerful
> force at my disposal.'
>
> German General Student on observing the initial landing, from
> Christopher Hibbert, *Arnhem*

Eventually, the Irish Guards made their advance, without adequate
air support. To avoid confusion in what would be a very crowded
airspace, the eleven squadrons of No. 83 Air Group, assigned to
the XXX Corps' attack, had been ordered to mount no combat
air patrol operations and had been told that no air strikes were
to be made within 20 miles (32km) of the airborne forces' flight
path. Again, this could have been avoided if the ground attack had
commenced at dawn before the airlift had left their bases in the
south and east of England. Elsewhere in the Market Garden area air
strikes had been conducted through the night of 16/17 September
by over 2,000 aircraft, hitting several targets in and around Arnhem
including Ede Barracks, Deelen airfield and, tragically, the Wolfheze
Asylum where many patients and staff were killed. On the morning
of the 17th more than 3,500 aircraft and gliders carrying the 82nd,
101st and 1st British Airborne Divisions took to the air and started
their journey to the continent. Half an hour before the arrival of
1st Airborne, the 186 men of 23rd Independent Company landed
in the Netherlands to carry out their pathfinder tasks of laying
out recognition panels on the drop zones and landing zones,
and setting up their Eureka homing equipment. Within half an
hour of the arrival of the pathfinder unit, the gliders carrying the

21. A Douglas C47 'Dakota' aircraft; the Dakota was the mainstay of paratroop and glider transport. (Courtesy of Tim Lynch)

Airlanding Brigade and the first wave of the divisional assets were touching down on LZs 'Z' and 'S' and followed by more than 140 transports carrying 1st Parachute Brigade at DZ 'X' at 1.50pm. A number of aircraft and glider combinations were lost to flak and mechanical failure – mostly glider tow ropes breaking – and a few aircraft missed their drop or landing zones, but generally it was a remarkably successful landing. Inevitably there was some confusion in the first hours; General Urquhart was informed, quite wrongly, that many of the reconnaissance jeeps had failed to arrive, forcing him to make an alternative plan for the *coup de main* sortie to the bridge. The glider carrying the commanding officer of the Border Regiment, Lieutenant Colonel Hadden, had aborted over England, so his second-in-command, Major Cousens, took over the battalion, but all of the units were delivered virtually intact – Frost's 2nd Battalion was able to assemble 95 per cent of its men within an hour of the drop and that seems to have been fairly typical of the infantry units. Overall, Urquhart had every reason to be pleased with the landing

22. 1st Parachute Brigade descending on Drop Zone (DZ) 'X' on the first day of the battle.

process. His Divisional HQ was established at 2.15pm. The various divisional assets – anti-tank batteries, engineers, the two batteries of 1st Airlanding Regiment units – concentrated quickly with little loss. The Airlanding Brigade set about the business of securing the landing zones while the RASC detachments collected supply containers and the field ambulance units prepared for casualties.

Urquhart, who had travelled by glider, was able to watch 1st Parachute Brigade assemble for their march into Arnhem, each battalion column accompanied by a troop of four 6 pounder guns from the Royal Artillery Airlanding anti-tank batteries. The battle of Arnhem was under way.

THE BATTLEFIELD
WHAT ACTUALLY HAPPENED?

The Attack Commences – Day One

1st Parachute Brigade begin to move off, along separate codenamed routes, towards the main objective: Arnhem Bridge; British 1st Airborne Division lands

2pm	XXX Corps' artillery barrage commences
	Guards Armoured Division moves off, encountering anti-tank guns, but air strikes allow them to continue advancing, although blockages in the road delay advance throughout the afternoon
3pm	2nd and 3rd battalions advance along Lion and Tiger routes respectively
3.30pm	1st Battalion moves off along Leopard route
	1 mile outside Wolfheze the Reconnaissance Squadron is ambushed by SS Kraft Battalion; they are unable to reach the objective and are forced to divert to Leopard route
	Brigadier Lathbury and General Urquhart join 3rd Battalion, facing heavy German resistance
	1st Battalion, warned by Reconnaissance Squadron, divert off the route, but meet heavy resistance and are unable to reach the bridge

7.30pm	2nd Battalion's A Company reaches the bridge with minimal casualties
	Attempts to cross the bridge are thwarted by resistance and a flamethrower attack; B Company and remaining companies are stopped short of their objectives
8pm	2nd Battalion's headquarters company reaches the main objective
Nightfall	1st and 3rd battalions forced to halt advance due to resistance; 3rd Battalion stop at Hartenstein Hotel
	Guards Armoured Division (XXX Corps) also halts advance for the night, having only progressed 6.2 miles during the afternoon
	SS Kraft Battalion ceases attack and withdraws to reform; the Germans have seized divisional plan earlier during the day, detailing objectives and the operation plan

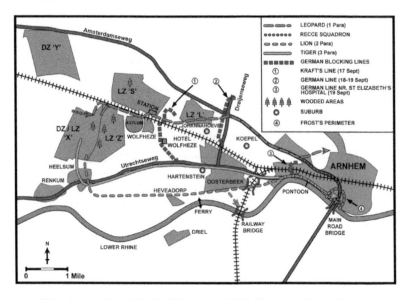

23. The Arnhem Battlefield, 17–19 September 1944. (Courtesy of Lloyd Clark, Arnhem)

THE NEBELWERFER

Literally 'fog thrower', the Nebelwerfer was the name given to a series of multiple tube rocket launchers to disguise their real function from the Allies. The most common type was a six-barrelled weapon which could fire High Explosive, Incendiary or smoke projectiles to a range of about 4 miles (7km). The crew would load the projectiles and then take cover at least 10 metres from the weapon during the firing process to avoid the fumes generated by the propellant. The Nebelwerfer could deliver an impressive concentration of fire in a very short period and was widely – and justifiably – feared by Allied troops in every theatre of war.

On Sunday 17 September, the 2nd and 3rd Parachute battalions moved off at about 3pm; the 3rd on the Utrechtseweg route – codenamed 'Tiger' and the 2nd along the riverside 'Lion' road. Brigadier Lathbury ordered 1st Battalion, who were to take a road to the north of the railway line – codenamed 'Leopard' – to remain at the drop zone for about half an hour; quite why is open to question. Lathbury's plan had not allowed for a specific brigade reserve and it is generally believed that he intended to send Lieutenant Colonel Dobie's 1st Battalion in the footsteps of either 2nd or 3rd, if either of them found a clear path to the bridge or to support either of them if they met strong resistance. Neither of these propositions is altogether convincing. Even if brigade communications were 100 per cent effective, it would take some time for 1st Battalion to come to the support of either of the other battalions if the Germans put up a fight, and since there was no mobile reconnaissance element allotted to either of the battalions there was no way of knowing if the road to the bridge was undefended save by marching there. More significantly, if Lathbury had really intended to give 1st Battalion a reserve role, why would he have assigned them to take the Leopard

81

route at all? A delay of half an hour would, at best, allow 2nd and 3rd battalions to penetrate only a quarter of the distance to the objective and in any case, according to the brigade plan, 1st Battalion were to occupy an area of high ground about 1 mile (1.5km) north of the bridge.

The first major blow to the divisional plan occurred just under a mile (about 1km) east of Wolfheze, when two of the reconnaissance jeeps ran into a German ambush in dense woodland by Major Kraft's SS battalion. Kraft was the commander of a training school which chiefly consisted of 17–19-year-old recruits. As the British arrived, Kraft threw his men into the battle and played an instrumental part in frustrating the British effort by disrupting Lathbury's brigade plan in its early stages. He wrote in his battle diary:

> … it would be wrong to play a purely defensive role and let the enemy gather his forces unmolested. Whilst it is not the rule to attack far superior forces, there are occasions when this must be done.
>
> From Christopher Hibbert, Arnhem

The balance of the Reconnaissance Squadron was drawn into a prolonged skirmish along the line of the railway and was clearly not going to be able to force its way to the objective. As soon as he heard that the Reconnaissance Squadron had been blocked, Lathbury sought out his battalion commanders, encouraging them to make the best speed they could to their objectives. He reached Lieutenant Colonel Fitch's 3rd Battalion, which was already facing some difficulty and was joined soon after by General Urquhart, who, aware that the Reconnaissance Squadron's *coup de main* strike had failed, had decided that he was too far away from the battle and had left his headquarters to see what he could do to hasten the advance. By this time the 3rd Battalion was under pressure from behind as well as being unable to make any progress to the front. Night was approaching and a decision was made to halt at the Hartenstein Hotel with a view to renewing the attack in the morning. Urquhart

24. The Hartenstein Hotel as seen from the tennis courts where German POWs were held. (Author photograph)

would have no further contact with his headquarters for the next day and a half.

While 3rd Battalion were running into an unexpectedly stout resistance, Lieutenant Colonel Dobie's 1st Battalion had met elements of the retreating Reconnaissance Squadron, who informed them of the situation. Dobie, realising that he had neither the time nor the force for a stiff fight, decided to move north through the woods to outflank the force which had stopped Major Freddie Gough's Reconnaissance Squadron. His leading company were able to brush aside some light resistance, but soon encountered a large German force with armoured support and were held up until nightfall. Meanwhile, Dobie's T Company diverted on to another road, but again met German armoured units, and so moved the axis of advance south of the road through more woodland, fighting continual small engagements but making little headway. By nightfall the battalion was spread across a large area, had suffered many casualties and were already running low on ammunition. Thus, the Reconnaissance Squadron and two of the three battalions assigned to the attacks had been stopped in their tracks several kilometres short of the bridge.

The 2nd Battalion under Frost, assigned to the Lion route, marched south from DZ 'X', passing through the village of Heelsum before turning east and advancing through the southern edge of Doorwerthsche woods. They met minor resistance from time to time which they either brushed aside or evaded. The battalion's A Company made straight for the road bridge, arriving at about 7.30pm, having encountered some armoured cars and infantry, but having lost only one man dead and a handful of wounded to enemy action. A single rifle section made a tentative attempt to cross the bridge but retired on finding opposition. A platoon attack was mounted, which also failed and further attempts became impractical due to a flamethrower igniting a store of ammunition or possibly petrol. Between intermittent explosions and the bridge paintwork catching fire, there was far too much light for a successful attack. During the night a small convoy of German trucks attempting to cross bridge was completely destroyed. Although this was a success in its own right, it must have been a cause for concern for Frost's men, since the convoy had come from the direction from which they expected reinforcements from the balance of the brigade. More encouragingly, Frost was able to make radio contact with Dobie, who decided to march to 2nd Battalion's aid through the night. However, Dobie's troops encountered continual resistance and became scattered in a series of fierce street actions; by dawn Dobie was in touch with only a fragment of his unit.

Frost's battalion plan had assigned B Company to take a pontoon bridge to the west of the main target, but they were delayed by an attempt to take an area of high wooded ground called Den Brink, from which the enemy were interfering with the battalion's advance. Frost had already been informed that the bridge had been partially dismantled, but thought 'it might still be possible to make some use of it'. Only the centre section of the bridge was missing, so if A Company were not strongly opposed it might be possible for the engineers attached to the battalion to use the remaining pontoon

25. A British M10 tank destroyer crossing a Bailey bridge. The M10 was a more heavily armoured and better-gunned variant of the Sherman, designed to offset the superior armament of the German Panther and Tiger tanks. Plans to build a Bailey bridge into the Airborne Division perimeter were abandoned as impractical.

sections to move troops across river and assault the south end of bridge. This turned out to be impractical, so the company halted for the night.

The remaining company had been sent to take the railway bridge, cross it and attack the southern end of the road bridge, but reached their objective only to see it blow up. Shortly afterwards a runner arrived from Frost, instructing the company commander to move on to his secondary objective, the German town headquarters.

By 8pm Frost's headquarter's company, with the mortar and machine gun platoons, had arrived at the main objective, where they were joined by 1st Brigade headquarters, about 130 men from the Royal Engineers and RASC, a dozen glider pilots, five anti-tank guns and Major Gough with two jeeps from his Reconnaissance Squadron. Frost now had a little over 700 men under his command,

THE 'WELBIKE'

The Welbike was a folding motorcycle with a two-stroke
engine specially designed by the research unit at Welwyn
– hence the name 'Wel'-bike. It was for airdropping
to resistance groups and despatch riders in parachute
operations, but many were used by other branches of
service. Designed to fit into a standard airdrop canister,
it had a range of over 62 miles (100km) on a single tank
and a top speed of about 64mph (40km/hour). Over 3,000
Welbikes were made in 1942–43.

and the arrival of a captured German truck full of ammunition must
have been a welcome addition, but there was no sign of the balance
of the brigade.

Having arrived at the bridge, Frost's men did not have to wait long
to be put to the test. A small convoy of German trucks was quickly
dealt with, but was soon followed by a column of German armoured
vehicles attacking through the wreckage:

> I had thought that the burning lorries would prove an obstacle to
> anything except a tank, but by now their fires were almost out and
> the leading armoured car was able to nose its way through a gap
> between them and accelerate away, undamaged, even by the necklace
> of mines we had laid during the night. The explosion of one mine
> seriously disturbed the crew, but three more were able to pass our
> ambush and move away at speed into the town. By the time the
> fourth one appeared, our anti-tank weapon crews had found the
> range and seven were soon disabled and burning before our eyes.
>
> John Frost, *A Drop Too Many*

The intensity of the fighting at the bridge made as much of an
impression on German soldiers as on the British ones:

The Battlefield: What Actually Happened?

> Starting from the rooftops, buildings collapsed like doll's houses. I did not see how anyone could live through this inferno. I felt truly sorry for the British.
>
> Private Horst Weber, from R. Kershaw,
> *It Never Snows in September*

While the three battalions of 1st Brigade were engaged in and around the town, the balance of the division continued with their tasks. Divisional headquarters moved into empty gliders on LZ 'Z' for the night. The final divisional diary entry for 17 September states 'operations proceeding to plan' and the entry at 6am on the 18th expresses the same opinion – 'During night, operations developed according to plan', but goes on to state that the battalions of 1st Brigade had encountered stiff resistance on the roads leading into Arnhem and that 7th King's Own Scottish Borderers (KOSBs) had met increasing opposition, but had cleared and secured DZ 'Y' for the drop of 4th Parachute Brigade. This was a rather optimistic analysis of the situation. The 1st and 3rd battalions were scattered some distance from the objective, and 2nd Battalion was at the bridge, but without two of its three rifle companies. The operation was very clearly not going according to plan at all, and the divisional commander was stranded with 3rd Battalion, some distance from his headquarters.

In reality, by nightfall on the 17th the Germans were already well on their way to victory, though that was not obvious to the staff of 1st Airborne Division. The main attacking force had been thoroughly disrupted and the objective, though denied to the Germans, had not been secured for the British. The fighting in the town had eased during the night as Major Kraft, aware that his job of disrupting the enemy's advance while covering the concentration of 9th Panzer Division was becoming increasingly difficult and realising that his own slender force was in danger of becoming as badly fragmented as his opposition, withdrew to reform his troops.

26. Landing Zone (LZ) 'Z' covered with Horsa gliders.

So far, the battle had not favoured Urquhart's men at all. The Germans had identified the British aims perfectly and could be confident that they would contain 1st Airborne while reinforcements were gathered and brought to the battle.

Although the fighting in the town was intense, there was relatively little interference from the Germans around the divisional area. In part this was because the German units available on the eastern aspect had been committed to preventing entry to Arnhem rather than attacking westward. The units to the west of the dropping and landing zones were less mobile, less capable and less committed. Attacks on the zones were not pressed hard, however they were not being mounted by combat formations, just ad hoc units of navy and Luftwaffe personnel with little or no infantry training and very limited amounts of artillery or armour.

The Battlefield: What Actually Happened?

The Germans, however, could afford to be patient. The British objectives were so obvious that even the capture of the entire 1st Airborne Division plan, complete with drop zones and order of battle from a crashed glider, did little more than confirm what they had already surmised. Not all of their assets were in a condition to be committed immediately and some of their units were of questionable value, but by dusk on 17 September they were rightly confident that victory was within reach.

Despite an efficient drop, the British 1st Airborne Division had not got off to a good start, and there were problems with the ground attack as well. The barrage in front of XXX Corps had commenced at 2pm and the Guards started their advance about half an hour later. The challenge of the terrain became apparent almost

27. A unit of Guards Armoured Division at Valkenswaard on the first day of the battle.

immediately. There was only one suitable road, so the Germans knew exactly where the thrust must come. Anti-tank guns deployed along the road knocked out about a dozen tanks and armoured cars on a stretch of less than 1,000 metres, blocking the road and making armoured crews very wary of advancing without infantry in front. Air support – now available since the transport aircraft were out of way – soon dealt with the immediate opposition, but the road needed to be cleared by engineers before the advance could continue. Progress thereafter was not quick and at dusk, when the forward elements of XXX Corps were only 6.2 miles (10km) from the start line, they harboured for the night. The Guards Armoured Division seems to have developed a general policy of not moving through the hours of darkness due to the loss of observation for air and artillery support and the possibility of confusion, however since the road north was the only real objective, it would surely have been difficult to get lost and the issue of visibility was same for both sides. More importantly, the practice of halting at dusk and resuming at dawn was widely understood by the Germans, who were able use the night for redeployment, reinforcement and re-supply, free from Allied interference. This might not have been a fatal flaw if the attack had been resumed at dawn, but this was not the case; throughout the entire Market Garden operation the Guards never moved off at dawn, and generally not until midday or later.

Appraising the Situation – Day Two

Units continue to head towards the Arnhem Bridge, but run into resistance

18 September	4.30am	3rd Battalion, 1st Brigade move towards Lion route
	6.30am	Frost's 2nd Battalion are under increasing pressure from German resistance
	7am	3rd Battalion's leading company nearly reaches 2nd Battalion at Arnhem Bridge, but is separated from the rest of the battalion

18 September		Divisional diary records growing German opposition in the Oosterbeek area
	8am	1st Battalion, 1st Parachute Brigade, march through Oosterbeek, towards Lion route, but encounter heavy German resistance
	9.15am	General Urquhart is still separated from divisional headquarters with 3rd Battalion; Brigadier Hicks arrives at the headquarters to assume temporary command
		Hicks sends South Staffordshires into Arnhem to provide support for the struggling battalions of 1st Parachute Brigade
	9.30am	2nd Battalion are attacked by Reconnaissance Battalion, 9th SS Panzer Division, however they are able to repulse the Germans after fighting for 2 hours
	10am	Supplies and reinforcements from 4th Brigade due; this drop is delayed due to poor weather
		All units in Arnhem face German attacks and resistance, including those units guarding the landing zones; many units are divided and weakened
	2.30pm	South Staffordshires run into difficulties and cannot reach 2nd Battalion at Arnhem Bridge
	3pm	Supply and 4th Brigade drop (originally due at 10am) takes place
		11th Battalion, 4th Brigade is diverted to support units in Arnhem
	5pm	Divisional headquarters moves into Hartenstein Hotel
	Nightfall	4th Brigade runs into difficulties
		1st Battalion halts 1km from Frost's 2nd Battalion
	11.30pm	South Staffordshires advance has been halted and their force is depleted; they report back to headquarters; the situation looks bleak

91

To the staff at Urquhart's headquarters, the tactical situation at dawn on Monday 18 September did not seem altogether bleak. The landing and drop zones were apparently secure, reinforcements and supplies were expected by 10am and another drive mounted into town could recover 1st Brigade and relieve Frost's 2nd Battalion at the bridge. On the other hand, the 7am entry in the divisional diary makes no mention of communication with 1st Brigade or with General Urquhart, but records growing opposition in the Oosterbeek area.

Urquhart's absence was becoming an increasing problem. His chief staff officer, Lieutenant Colonel Charles MacKenzie, was doing what he could, but it was fast becoming clear that major changes would have to be made to the divisional plan.

By 9.15am, Brigadier Hicks had arrived at divisional headquarters and assumed command. Hicks was informed that Frost had arrived at the bridge and that 1st and 3rd battalions were heavily engaged, but he had limited resources for renewing the battle since the South Staffordshires – the only unit that could possibly be reassigned – was missing two rifle companies and half of its support company due to the shortage of airlift capacity on the 17th. After a consultation with MacKenzie, Hicks decided to send the Staffordshires into Arnhem to link up with 1st Brigade. Hicks was in an impossible position; given that Urquhart might return to his headquarters at any moment, he was unwilling to make radical alterations to the divisional plan and probably had no discretion to do so. Even if he had wanted to do so communications within the division and with Second Army and London were inadequate, the intelligence picture was not good, the Reconnaissance Squadron was already badly damaged and was, in any case, too vulnerable for operations against the armoured opposition which now faced the division on all sides. By 2.30pm it became apparent that the Staffordshires could not hope to reach Frost and that Hicks would have to dispatch more men to the fight if the objective was to be secured.

This might yet have brought success if 4th Brigade had landed as scheduled at 10am, but the drop was delayed by bad weather in

28. Brigadier P.H.W. Hicks – Brigadier Hicks took command of the division during Urquhart's enforced absence from his headquarters during the early stages of the battle.

England and Hackett's force of 2,000 men did not arrive until shortly after 3pm. By this time the Germans had started to make some headway against the Border Regiment and the KOSBs guarding the landing zones. Throughout Monday morning they had both repulsed several attacks. The Border Regiment had suffered casualties from a German airstrike just before the second lift was due to arrive and B Company, stationed at Renkum brickworks to prevent German reinforcements coming along the Utrechtseweg, had come under severe pressure, and were forced to withdraw to rejoin the battalion at around 2.30pm, but damage to transport forced them to abandon two anti-tank guns and a substantial amount of ammunition. In the north corner of DZ 'Y' a detached platoon of KOSBs was forced to surrender after heavy casualties.

Despite these setbacks, 4th Brigade's drop was achieved with little loss. Shortly afterwards, Hackett was met by MacKenzie, who informed him that Brigadier Hicks had taken command and that 11th Battalion was to be removed from 4th Brigade and sent into Arnhem to support the units already engaged. Although he recognised that 11th Battalion, being the unit that had dropped closest to the town, was the best choice, Hackett was unhappy about the arrangement. It completely destabilised his brigade plan which had been focused on controlling an area to the north of Arnhem. The validity of the plan was in question if the objective could not be secured, which was by no means certain; equally, there was no guarantee that one more battalion would be enough to change the course of the battle and Hackett might be losing a third of his combat strength to no good purpose.

Meanwhile, the gliders carrying the balance of the divisional assets and the remaining companies of the South Staffordshires had made successful landings on zones 'Z' and 'X', despite an attempted intervention by the Luftwaffe. Aware that reinforcements and supplies had to be landed somewhere and with the benefit of an hour's warning from the garrison at Dunkirk, the Luftwaffe mounted an attack with about ninety aircraft, but had been unable to make much impression on the landings. A number of gliders had been damaged by enemy fire in the air and on the ground, and a few had collided with gliders from the previous day's lift. Unfortunately, the supply drop to zone 'L' by Stirling bombers had not gone so well. The majority of the 80 tons of food and ammunition had been collected by the Germans who had gained control over most of the area.

By nightfall, 4th Brigade had become seriously disrupted. Hackett's 10th Battalion had remained on the landing area protecting the field ambulance and casualties, while 156th Battalion moved eastward along the line of the railway until they came to LZ 'L' – now firmly in German hands – and were prevented from making any further progress. Exhaustion soon became a major factor, especially for those standing guard through the night:

The Battlefield: What Actually Happened?

My eyes would strain into the darkness until my lids were too heavy to stay open any longer and I'd nod off, only to wake, startled out of my wits and straining around, expecting Jerries everywhere … It was lucky I hadn't had to use my rifle during the night for I couldn't even see through the barrel for dirt.

Anonymous soldier of 156th Battalion, from Christopher Hibbert, Arnhem

Hackett's entire brigade area was, to use his own term, 'busy' throughout the day. He had asked for, and been given, command of the KOSBs to ensure the security of the landing areas, but they were already heavily committed and could not be moved to meet any new threats. It was not until midnight that Hackett was able to meet with Hicks, and when he did, the encounter did not go too well. Hackett was unhappy about the general situation which he described as being 'grossly untidy'. He was concerned that units

29. British Airborne troops dug-in behind a hedge.

and detachments were widely scattered and that there was no clear policy to concentrate the division.

Another difficult aspect of the situation was that Hackett had seniority and had not been made aware of Urquhart's decision that, should he be put out of action himself, command of the division should pass to Lathbury and then only to Hicks if Lathbury was lost as well. However, after a tempestuous meeting, Hackett and Hicks agreed on a new plan. Hackett would lead 4th Brigade to Koepel north of the railway line and then advance into the town. This was on the assumption that he would then be to the left of 1st Parachute Brigade and that both brigades would then make a concerted attack, with the objective of relieving Frost at the bridge. Unbeknown to either brigadier was that 1st Brigade was no longer a coherent formation.

During Sunday night, Lieutenant Colonel Dobie's 1st Parachute Battalion had passed through Oosterbeek, but the leading company had been stopped by a strong enemy position at a railway bridge. The company was ordered to disengage and follow the rest of the battalion, which was already missing one company and most of the anti-tank, mortar and machine gun assets which had become detached during the action at the Amsterdamseweg. The battalion now moved south towards the Lion route used by 2nd Battalion the day before. Steady progress was made until about 8am when Dobie's battalion encountered a strong German force. Despite the presence of enemy armour and his own shortage of anti-tank weapons, if Dobie was to make any contribution to the main objective of the operation he really had little choice other than to attack. This proved to be a challenging undertaking, and although the battalion made some distance, it was a slow and costly business and by nightfall they were still more than a kilometre from Frost's increasingly perilous position.

Meanwhile, Fitch's 3rd Battalion, along with Urquhart and Lathbury, had made a similar move. Believing that the road ahead was strongly held and that he could not afford the time, casualties and ammunition for a fight that would have little bearing on

The Battlefield: What Actually Happened?

Frost's situation, at 4.30am Fitch led his troops south to the Lion route. By 7am his leading company were little more than a kilometre from the bridge, but had become separated from the rest of the unit. Somewhere behind them lay Fitch with A Company, but they too had become separated from the balance of the battalion and had the added responsibility of being accompanied by both the divisional and brigade commanders. At this point Fitch encountered an enemy force, which, though they chose not to make an attack, prevented any further progress, so he had little choice but to lay up until evening before slipping away in the hope of finding some portion of the rest of the battalion. He was at least relieved of the burden of Urquhart and Lathbury, both of whom were naturally anxious to rejoin their respective headquarters and had decided to attempt to do so on foot.

Monday had not gone well for the division as a whole, though the drops and landings had gone reasonably well, the drive into town by 11th Battalion and the remainder of the South Staffordshires had ground to a halt well short of its target and there had been increasing pressure from the west.

30. Arnhem Bridge. Although it was demolished by Allied bombing after the battle it was rebuilt in a very similar form and looks little different today from its appearance in 1944. (Author photograph)

The situation at the bridge had seen no improvement, but had remained fairly stable. Frost had made contact with his B Company and ordered them to join him, but increasing German activity forced them to fight their way into the battalion position and when they arrived at 6.30am there were only seventy of them left. A party from 3rd Battalion managed to join the defence, but the balance of the company was surrounded and forced to surrender in the vicinity of St Elizabeth's Hospital.

The situation was not yet critical. The bridge was still denied to the enemy, forcing the Germans to move reinforcements from the Nijmegen sector by means of a ferry at Pannerden, some kilometres to the east. The possibility of another attempt to secure the southern end of the bridge was considered, but rejected since it would inevitably cost lives and would probably force a reduction in the perimeter. The supply situation was not desperate given that the defenders expected the imminent arrival of XXX Corps.

At about 9.30am the defenders heard the sound of many vehicles approaching from the south and initially assumed that relief had

LANDMARKS

Several battlefield landmarks still stand in Arnhem and Oosterbeek; most of the mature trees in the parkland around the Hartenstein Hotel still bear the marks of battle, including at least two with holes clean through the trunk. The bridge was bombed in October 1944, but looks substantially the same today. The Hartenstein Hotel now houses the battlefield museum, and the Tafelberg, the Hotel Dreyeroord (known to the British as 'The White House'), Oosterbeek church and Kate ter Horst's house which sits next door to it are little changed. Most of the houses that lie in the 'cauldron' area are from the nineteenth century and, though they have obviously been repaired, many are easily recognisable from contemporary photographs and newsreel.

The Battlefield: What Actually Happened?

31. Known to the troops of the Airborne Division as 'The White House', the Hotel Dreyeroord was the scene of fierce combat through the middle and latter stages of the battle. (Author photograph)

arrived. They soon saw that it was not the Irish Guards but actually elements of the Reconnaissance Battalion of 9th SS Panzer Division, newly returned from Nijmegen. The Germans advanced and were badly beaten in an attack lasting for about 2 hours. British casualties were not heavy, but there was an enormous expenditure of ammunition which could not be made good unless physical contact was made with the division.

By 5pm divisional headquarters had moved into the Hartenstein Hotel, where it would remain for the rest of the operation. There was now very little that Brigadier Hicks could do to influence the battle. All of the troops that could be diverted to Arnhem had been committed, but there was little to show for their sacrifice. His two choices were to continue to pursue the original objective or to attempt to form a strong perimeter based on the current position of the division around Oosterbeek. It is important to remember that at this juncture, Hicks, and everyone around him, had every reason to believe that XXX Corps would turn up in the very near future and that the Arnhem Bridge was still, therefore, of paramount

99

importance. He must have realised that German forces in the area were larger and of better quality than had been expected and that the day's supply drop had not been very successful, but there was very little he could do other than proceed with the original plan as far as possible.

By dusk on Monday 18 September he was aware that the second advance into Arnhem had failed to reach the bridge and that the units were badly scattered, but he knew the troops were of the highest calibre and might have reasonably expected that a considerable number of men would find their way to their units or to the divisional area. Furthermore, he now had virtually all of the division on the ground and could be confident that his force would put up a stern fight which, at the very least, would prevent the Germans from moving units to oppose XXX Corps. However, he did not become aware of just how heavily the units in question had suffered until 11.30pm, when a South Staffordshires officer reached divisional headquarters and informed him that the Staffordshires advance had been halted and that they were not in touch with either 1st or 3rd battalions, but that they seemed to be pinned down some distance from Frost's 2nd Battalion and had been reduced to no more than about 150 men. He was further informed – quite wrongly – that Urquhart and Lathbury were with 2nd Battalion.

Hicks now had no force that he could commit to the battle until the arrival of the Polish Brigade and therefore no prospect of being able to reinforce or relieve Frost, and in any case the arrival of the Poles would almost inevitably be offset by German reinforcements. The only course of action open was to try to form a strong perimeter around Oosterbeek and hope that XXX Corps would be able to build a Bailey bridge across the river.

The position was certainly grim – poor communications were preventing adequate air support, supply drops were obviously going badly and unlikely to improve, and the plight of the casualties and of the local population was becoming an issue. Water was becoming very scarce and the airborne troops were putting a strain on civilian

32. British Airborne troops carrying the unloved Sten gun on a patrol in the Oosterbeek area.

food stores. Local resistance volunteers who had joined the fight were also becoming understandably concerned about reprisals if the British were defeated. Although the people of Arnhem and Oosterbeek were largely delighted at the arrival of the British, not everyone was happy; Lieutenant Colonel Frost encountered some resistance when he roused the owner of a house which overlooked the bridge:

> He was not at all happy about billeting soldiers. The Germans, he said, had gone and he would much prefer us to march on after them. When I convinced him that the Germans were still very much there and furthermore that we didn't merely want billets but proposed to fortify the house in readiness for a battle, he retired to the cellar quite horrified.
>
> John Frost, *A Drop Too Many*

Opposition Increases – Day Three

All units in and around Arnhem face opposition

19 September	7.25am	General Urquhart returns to divisional headquarters
		Urquhart orders 4th Brigade to seize the high ground around LZ 'L' and then move to Koepel, north of Arnhem; then orders KOSBs to take the village of Lichtenbeek
		The units run into heavy opposition
	3pm	Urquhart, realising 4th Brigade is unable to renew the attack, orders a withdrawal; units begin to disengage
		4th Brigade's path to re-joining the division is blocked by a steep railway embankment; most of the brigade manage to pass through a tunnel
		British supply drop is seized by Germans
		Units in the town are separated from each other and face more fighting; they are unable to reach the bridge or recover the landing zones

The Battlefield: What Actually Happened?

| 19 September | 7.30pm | 4th Brigade, having failed to fully disengage, finds its path blocked by the Germans and are pinned down |
| | 11.30pm | 4th Brigade's headquarters and 156th Battalion move to a pre-arranged area, but are still distant from the divisional area |

Hicks was relieved of the responsibility of making further divisional decisions by the return of Urquhart at 7.25am on Tuesday 19 September. By this time the division was engaged in three distinct actions; Frost's troops at the bridge, the units attempting to force a passage into Arnhem and the remaining elements of the division spread across the countryside from Oosterbeek to the drop zones. In an attempt to regain the initiative, Hackett was now ordered to seize high ground around LZ 'L' and then move on to take Koepel to the north of Arnhem with 10th and 156th battalions and direct the KOSBs – still attached to 4th Brigade – to attack the village of Lichtenbeek. This would be followed by a brigade attack which would bring them onto the left flank of the remnants of 1st Brigade, the South Staffordshires and 10th Battalion. The KOSBs were unable to make much progress and were obliged to retire to Johannahoeve. Poor signals and stiff opposition with armoured support led to an inability to coordinate efforts or take account of developments. The 156th and 10th battalions made some progress, but strong resistance and a shortage of ammunition forced them to come to a halt and then to retrace their steps toward LZ 'L'. Unfortunately, 10th Battalion arrived shortly after the landing of the glider element of 1st Polish Brigade. At the same time a company of the KOSBs, sent by Lieutenant Colonel Payton-Reid to assist with unloading, approached from the other direction and there was a great deal of friendly fire as the Poles disembarked their jeeps, guns and carriers. The process was further hampered by German air attacks which inflicted many casualties and the loss of yet more equipment and ammunition.

33. Two British airborne soldiers – one apparently wearing a signaller's headset – man a slit-trench among the redundant jeeps and trailers.

By early afternoon it had become clear that the 4th Brigade attack could not be renewed, so Urquhart ordered Hackett to retire into the divisional position and take up a position to protect against attacks from the east. The brigade started to disengage at 3pm, but withdrawing in the face of a competent and well-organised enemy is easier said than done. In order to join the division, Hackett's force would have to negotiate a steep railway embankment. The men could cross – though at some risk since there were now German troops scattered throughout the area – but the brigade transport could only cross at either the Wolfheze or Oosterbeek stations. The latter was strongly held, so Hackett planned an attack on the former, but was informed by local resistance that elements of an ad hoc German formation, 'Division Tettau', were approaching from the west. Fortunately a small tunnel through the embankment was discovered and a sizeable proportion of the brigade's transport was able to pass through, but it seems the tunnel was too narrow to allow the passage of carriers and a good deal of precious equipment had to be abandoned. The chaos of battle is summed up by the experience of Andrew Milbourne's Vickers gun team, who met resistance at a crossroads near Wolfheze:

> Yells and whistles filled the air and machine guns opened fire. I noticed before I hugged the ground that one of the enemy guns was about 200 yards in front and to our left flank. My officer asked if I had seen anything and when I pointed this gun out to him ordered my gun section into action. Grasping the tripod I ran across the road, diving headlong into a very convenient ditch. Cautiously I raised my head searching for a position for my gun.

Milbourne's gun team were immediately thrust into the thick of the battle:

> Everywhere we turned or moved we were swept with a withering fire. Dead lay all around, wounded were crying for water. Groans and shrieks of pain filled the air. Time and again they overran our positions and had to be driven out with the bayonet. During this fighting my gun was never out of action.
>
> From Christopher Hibbert, *Arnhem*

At much the same time, the day's supply drop was delivered as arranged on the dedicated site 'V' about 1,000 metres north-east of Koepel; however, this area was now in German hands. Troops on the ground did their utmost to signal the aircrews that this was the case, laying out triangular yellow panels and discharging yellow smoke, but the pilots had strict orders to ignore ground signal for fear of a German ruse and very little material was recovered.

Arnhem 1944

34. Vickers guns of a British machine gun platoon.

Matters went from bad to worse for 4th Brigade who had failed to fully disengage. By 7.30pm most of the formation had moved to a position south of the railway line only to find their path blocked by the enemy and that they were now effectively pinned down. It was very difficult to make any sort of progress in the dark. By 11.30pm brigade headquarters and 156th Battalion had managed to move to a pre-arranged position, but were still some distance from the divisional area.

Things were no better in the town. The headquarters of Hicks' 1st Airlanding Brigade had been able to regain some communication with the South Staffordshires and reported that the force in that area comprising elements of the Staffordshires, 1st, 3rd and 11th parachute battalions, and a party of glider pilots now amounted

106

35. 1st Airlanding Regiment in action at Oosterbeek.

to only about 440 men of all ranks. Any prospect of reaching the bridge had gone. Throughout the afternoon, small parties and odd individuals from these battalions, separated from their units, had made their way westward in search of the remainder of the division. A number had found themselves close to the river and in front of the artillery, where they were promptly rounded up by Lieutenant Colonel William Thompson who deployed them to protect his guns. These men were briefly known as 'Thompson Force' from the traditional British practice of calling ad hoc units by the name of their commander, later renamed 'Lonsdale Force' after the officer from 4th Brigade appointed to take charge.

By now it was abundantly clear that 1st Airborne Division could not hope to recover any of the landing zones. Urquhart was asked for a new drop zone for the Polish Brigade and he chose an area slightly to the east of the village of Driel on the south side of the river in the hope that the Poles would be able to secure the area and thus form a bridgehead for XXX Corps on either side of the Neder Rhine.

This was not as optimistic as it might sound; there had, at last, been some communication with Second Army. At 10.15am Urquhart was informed that the leading elements of XXX Corps had arrived at Grave. The operation was well behind schedule, but at last relief was now less than 18.6 miles (30km) away and there was therefore still a good chance that 1st Airborne might be relieved and a bridgehead achieved even if the main objective was lost.

36. Elements of XXX Corps held up on the exposed road to Arnhem.

Waiting for Reinforcements – Day Four

20 September		
		2nd Battalion at Arnhem Bridge struggles to hold the objective
	8am	Urquhart orders Divisional 'O' Group to assess the situation
	8.20am	Divisional headquarters make radio contact with 1st Parachute Brigade's headquarters at the bridge; 2nd Battalion are desperate for reinforcements; Urquhart informs them that these are not forthcoming and they have to wait for XXX Corps
	9.30am	Intelligence receives a signal that XXX Corps are experiencing strong resistance south of Nijmegen, but intend to attack at the bridge at 1pm
		The Germans mount a series of attacks and artillery bombardments
	1pm	10th Battalion joins the division, having suffered heavy losses; Lieutenant Colonel Smyth informs Urquhart that 4th Brigade's headquarters and 156th Battalion are surrounded
	2pm	A supply drop takes place, but few containers are collected
		Frost's Battalion continues to request support and reinforcements at the bridge
	5pm	Another more successful supply drop takes place
	6.15pm	German Tiger tanks and reconnaissance vehicle cross the bridge; Allied units are forced to surrender
		156th Battalion breaks through to divisional area, having suffered heavy losses

Urquhart ordered a Divisional 'O' (Operations) Group for 8am on Wednesday 20 September, to get a better understanding of the strength of the units and in the hope of imposing some degree of control over the battle. At 8.20am divisional headquarters established radio contact with Major Hibbert of 1st Parachute Brigade's headquarters at the bridge, where Frost's force were still holding on with incredible tenacity but were desperate for

JEDBURGH TEAM

These were groups of three of four men trained to arrange liaison with local resistance movements. The team assigned to operations in Arnhem – codenamed 'Claude' - consisted of two American specialists, Lieutenant Todd and Staff Sergeant Scott and a Netherlands officer, Captain Groenwoed. Like the rest of the Airborne Division they were plagued by radio communications problems, largely, it seems, due to the high concentration of certain metal in the soil, but they were able to make intermittent contact with London and, eventually, XXX Corps.

reinforcements, ammunition, food and a surgical team. However, Urquhart was forced to inform Hibbert that he could not expect any help at all from the division and would have to look to XXX Corps for relief. This was not a forlorn hope. Some time before 9.30am, the Phantom (intelligence) unit attached to the division received a signal that XXX Corps were still south of Nijmegen and experiencing strong resistance, but that an attack to secure the bridge was to be made at 1pm. If successful, the leading elements of the ground offensive would be less than 9.3 miles (15km) from Arnhem.

From 9.30am onward the Germans mounted a succession of attacks and artillery bombardments throughout the divisional area. German pressure was intense and the airborne troops had little in the way of effective anti-tank weapons:

> It was impossible to tell how many tanks there were and I don't think we ever disabled one for we never saw the crew get out. At about 1130 the Piat ammunition gave out. The tanks came up and our men were being killed one after the other … We could hear the call of 'stretcher-bearers' all the time.

> Major R. Cain, 2nd South Staffordshires,
> from Christopher Hibbert, *Arnhem*

The Battlefield: What Actually Happened?

Shortly after 1pm Lieutenant Colonel Ken Smyth's 10th Battalion were able to join the division. Heavy casualties and extreme exhaustion took their toll of all the units; General Urquhart saw the remnants of 10th Battalion arrive at the Oosterbeek perimeter, with only sixty men. 'The men were exhausted, filthy and bleeding, their discipline was immaculate.' Smyth was able to tell Urquhart that 4th Brigade headquarters and 156th Battalion had been surrounded but that Hackett was intending to make an attack to break through to join the division at the earliest opportunity.

At 2pm there was another attempt to drop supplies, but the perimeter was already so small that only a modest amount of material was collected and infiltration between the units of the division meant that it was becoming a hazardous business to pick up any containers that fell onto open ground. A second drop at 5pm, however, was rather more successful.

As the day wore on the division received several signals from the bridge, each asking for information about the arrival of the Poles

37. *British casualties receiving attention from American airborne medics on the road to Nijmegen.*

38. Airborne troops recovering supplies after a drop. Most of the metal containers and wicker hampers fell into German hands.

or the progress of XXX Corps. Relentless German pressure at the bridge meant a steady accumulation of casualties, including Colonel Frost himself, '… there was a sudden crash beside us. I was thrown several feet and I found myself lying face downwards on the ground with pain in both my legs.' In the middle of the afternoon the division was informed that Frost had been wounded and that Major Gough of the Reconnaissance Squadron was now in command at the bridge.

Gough was confident that the toehold at the bridge could be held for another night, but that relief must arrive in the very near future or the troops would simply be blown out of the handful of houses that formed their perimeter. He also reported that in his view the bridge could not be blown because the charges and detonation wiring that the Germans had installed had been destroyed by the fire on the bridge on Sunday night. The fact remained, however, that the force at the bridge could no longer deny passage to the enemy. At 6.15pm a platoon of four Tiger tanks and a reconnaissance vehicle had crossed the bridge from north to south with impunity because the defenders no longer had any anti-tank weapons. This was an ominous sign in itself. Surrounded and under continual attack, the beleaguered force at the bridge eventually ran out of ammunition and were obliged to surrender:

> The SS men were very polite and complimentary about the battle we had fought, but the bitterness I felt was unassuaged. No living enemy had beaten us. The battalion was unbeaten yet, but they could not have much chance with no ammunition, no rest and no positions from which to fight.
>
> John Frost, *A Drop Too Many*

The German command obviously felt that they could defeat Urquhart's division with the tools to hand and could spare four heavy tanks for the force confronting XXX Corps' advance. Shortly after the reception of this signal, Brigadier Hackett was at last able to break through to the divisional area, but 156th Battalion had been reduced to only sixty men.

The Bridge is Lost – Day Five

The Polish Brigade arrive and attempt to cross the river

21 September	1am	Urquhart's headquarters receive a signal that Guards Armoured Division intend to attack at first light
	9am	Urquhart holds a conference to assess remaining strength and deployment of division
		KOSBs and the Border Regiment are under attack; 64th Medium Regiment retaliate with heavy fire to support the units
	10am	Oosterbeek is heavily bombarded by German fire; the divisional ammunition dump is set alight
	12.45pm	An Allied supply run suffers from heavy opposition by enemy fighters
	4pm	Another Allied supply run takes place

21 September	5.15pm	Polish Brigade begins their parachute drop with little resistance and quickly establishes headquarters
		2nd Polish Battalion moves to southern terminus of Heveadorp ferry
		3rd Polish Battalion moves across river from Oosterbeek church
	5.25pm	KOSBs are attacked and their position overrun; they counterattack to restore position, but suffer heavy losses
	9.30pm	Poles try to improvise rafts to cross the river
	9.44pm	Divisional headquarters report no contact with the forces at the bridge for 24 hours

Shortly after 1am Urquhart's headquarters received a signal that the Guards Armoured Division would 'go flat out' at first light. The recipients of the message must have wondered what had prevented the Guards from attacking through the night, though they may not have been aware that Nijmegen Bridge had fallen before dusk.

The divisional area had by now coalesced around Oosterbeek. Of the nine infantry battalions which had landed on 11 and 18 September, only the Border Regiment, stretched thinly along the entire western aspect of the perimeter, had anything like enough strength to retain a proper battalion structure. The eastern and northern aspects were not really bound by a formed line of units, but a collection of posts manned by elements of battalions or of divisional troops – engineers, signallers, RASC detachments and the glider pilots.

Determined to ensure that something would be salvaged from the operation, Urquhart focused his attention on the divisional perimeter. The bridge force had still been holding out at 4.15am, according to his information, but there was really nothing he could do to help there. He held a conference at 9am to ensure the best use of the remaining strength of the division and to create a viable command structure. The western aspect would now be commanded

39. The Germans failed to demolish the Nijmegen Bridge before it was seized by an audacious and heroic assault in broad daylight by US paratroops.

by Brigadier Hicks, with the remaining men of the Border Regiment, KOSBs, 21st Independent Company, engineers, the Reconnaissance Squadron and some of the glider pilots.

The eastern aspect would come under Hackett and would comprise the rest of the glider pilots, 10th and 156th Parachute battalions, the guns of 1st Airlanding Regiment, along with another party formed of mislaid men from 1st, 3rd, and 11th battalions, and the South Staffordshires, now named Lonsdale Force after the second-in-command of the 11th Battalion who, though wounded during the landing of 4th Brigade, had taken command of the party during a ferocious firefight the previous day.

By the time Urquhart was holding his conference, the KOSBs and the Border Regiment were already under attack from infantry and armour in the west, but in a rare turn of good fortune the division had now established contact with 64th Medium Regiment who laid down heavy concentrations of fire to disrupt the German formations.

The German artillery did not stand idle and the Oosterbeek area came under heavy fire, resulting in the divisional ammunition dump being set alight shortly after 10am. The ammunition supply was not yet critical, but it was certainly unsatisfactory. This was remedied to some degree by two more supply runs; one at 12.45pm which suffered heavily from enemy fighters and another at 4pm which was rather more successful, although actually gathering and distributing supplies was becoming more and more difficult as small parties of Germans and snipers infiltrated through the British lines. Water was, if anything, more critical. The Germans had cut off the supply and cisterns and radiators had been drained or destroyed by gunfire.

At 5.15pm two battalions and the headquarters of the Polish Brigade started their drop near Driel. There was surprisingly little action from the Germans and the brigade was able to muster and establish their headquarters with surprisingly few casualties. The 2nd Polish Battalion moved to the southern terminus of the Heveadorp ferry while the 3rd Polish Battalion deployed across the river from Oosterbeek church. The ferry itself was no longer available – it had been put out of action by its operator who had observed the Germans take the Westerbouwing Heights, a modest piece of high ground which overlooked both the ferry and the Oosterbeek perimeter. The Germans felt the strain of the battle as well:

> This was a harder battle than any I had fought in Russia. It was constant, close-range, hand-to-hand fighting. The English were everywhere. The streets, for the most part, were narrow, sometimes not more than 15 feet wide, and we fired at each other from only yards away.
>
> Alfred Ringdorf, 9th SS Panzer Division, from R. Kershaw,
> *It Never Snows in September*

The Battlefield: What Actually Happened?

The question now was how to get the Poles across the river and into action. Urquhart's chief engineer, Lieutenant Colonel Eddie Myers, set his mind to the problem and at 9.30pm was able to tell his general that a party had been sent down to the river to improvise rafts from some of the now-redundant jeep trailers that were scattered across the divisional area.

Meanwhile, Captain Zwolanski, the divisional headquarters Polish liaison officer, swam across the river and urged General Sosabowski to expedite the transfer of Polish troops into the perimeter, asking that the Poles do whatever they could to improvise rafts for the crossing, though little could be achieved by the Poles on the south bank or the engineers on the north due to a shortage of materials and the intensity of German fire.

Several attacks were made around the perimeter through the day, particularly on the eastern aspect. Most of these were supported by tanks and assault guns, requiring some local counterattacks to retain critical points. At 5.25pm the KOSBs

40. Oosterbeek parish church at the base of the perimeter. The house of Kate ter Horst in the background was used as a hospital. (Author photograph)

117

41. Temporary grave of an unidentified British airborne soldier.

were heavily attacked and their position was reported as overrun. The situation was restored by a counterattack at close quarters, although casualties were heavy and the battalion was now reduced to 150 men of all ranks. Little more than an hour later, Lonsdale Force near Oosterbeek church was attacked, but they repulsed the enemy, which seems to have been the general pattern of the day. The Germans did not make a concerted effort at any point or at any time and were content to keep the Airborne Division contained while their artillery steadily reduced the numbers and the morale of the defenders. By 9.44pm divisional headquarters reported to General Browning that there had been no contact with the defenders of the Arnhem Bridge for 24 hours: clearly the bridge was lost, and with it any prospect of making a rapid crossing of the Neder Rhine.

No Way Across – Day Six

22 September		
		Polish Brigade is unable to cross the river
		4th Brigade, Lonsdale Force are heavily attacked through the night. Attacks elsewhere throughout the divisional area, but perimeter remains fairly static
		Reports reach divisional headquarters that the Polish Brigade is unable to cross the river
	6am	Urquhart learns that Guards Armoured Division has halted north of Nijmegen and that 43rd Division intends to renew the advance at first light
	c.7am	Browning suggests that Urquhart should 'withdraw or cross the ferry' if necessary
	11.20am	Intelligence reports that a two-brigade attack was going to be launched to rescue Polish Brigade
	Afternoon	Attack cancelled, but Polish Brigade attempt a crossing, which is called off whilst in progress due to enemy fire

Lonsdale Force had been heavily attacked through night, but still retained their position. Elsewhere there had been a succession of minor attacks and infiltrations, but the perimeter was largely unchanged. Shortly before dawn Lieutenant Colonel George Stevens, the liaison staff officer attached to the Polish Brigade, arrived at divisional headquarters with the information that Polish Brigade headquarters and two of the brigade's three battalions were ensconced to the south of the river, but were currently unable to make a crossing, though they were trying to find means of doing so. A little after 6am another signal arrived from Browning's headquarters, informing Urquhart that the Guards Armoured Division had halted north of Nijmegen and that 43rd Division would renew the advance at first light, making for the Oosterbeek ferry – presumably the Heveadorp ferry which was now out of commission. Another signal an hour or so later reported that 43rd Division had been ordered to 'take all risks to effect relief'

42. Vehicles of XXX Corps crossing the bridge at Nijmegen.

but that if he felt the situation demanded, Urquhart should 'withdraw to or cross the ferry'. This rather suggests a certain lack of understanding of the situation on the part of Browning. Even if the ferry had been operable, it would hardly have been adequate for the needs of a division, even one so severely depleted as 1st Airborne, and it would have been terribly vulnerable to enemy fire. As soon as the Germans saw that the British were attempting to withdraw they would have concentrated their fire on the ferry and committed their infantry and armour to cut the perimeter at the riverbank or at least to prevent an orderly retreat.

Early in the day a troop of armoured cars from 2nd Household Cavalry had managed to reach the Polish Brigade under cover of fog, but no further reinforcements would arrive until the evening, though the Phantom unit attached to divisional headquarters received a signal at 11.20am that a two-brigade attack was about to be launched with the intention of making contact. In the meantime, Lieutenant Colonel MacKenzie crossed the river to see Sosabowski. The Poles were eager to help in any way they could, but when MacKenzie visited the headquarters of 43rd Division shortly afterwards he was struck by what he felt was a distinct lack of urgency. By mid-afternoon Urquhart had established direct radio contact with Sosabowski's headquarters and was able to arrange a crossing covered by a company-level dawn attack southward by the Border Regiment. It was not expected that more than 150 men would be able to join the division that night due to the shortage of boats. Demands within the divisional area led to the cancellation of the Border Regiment's projected attack but the Poles still tried to make a crossing; however, the operation had only delivered fifty-three men before enemy fire forced Sosabowski to abandon the attempt.

Under Fire – Day Seven

Continuous German attacks on the perimeter make it difficult to mount an offensive

23 September

7.30am	Germans shell the divisional area, targeting gliders; British artillery responds
8.40am	Glider pilots and 10th Battalion are forced to retreat from their defensive positions within the houses of Arnhem
	Strong attacks are launched on north-east corner of the perimeter; 43rd Division are unable to cross the river
	Border Regiment and Polish paratroopers repel attacks in south-west corner of the perimeter
	Attacks continue; a plan is formed to rescue the Poles and forces on the other side of the river during the following night

By 7.30am the Germans were shelling the divisional area, particularly around the headquarters at the Hartenstein Hotel, and within an hour the glider pilots in 4th Brigade's sector were the target of a heavy attack. The guns of 64th Regiment on the far side of the river opened fire but by 8.40am both the glider pilots and 10th Battalion

had been forced out of the houses they occupied and had taken to trenches in the gardens.

As the morning wore on there was a strong attack on the north-east corner of the perimeter and the leading elements of 43rd Division could be seen on the south bank of the river, but there was no means of getting them across to Oosterbeek due to the lack of boats and the intensity of German fire. An attack on the south-west corner of the perimeter was driven away by the Border Regiment and the detachment of Polish paratroopers. In the course of the day the Germans made little impression on the perimeter, but now that 43rd Division was so close, it was only a matter of time before a concerted attempt was made to cut the airborne pocket off from the riverbank and close their only means of escape. Near-continual combat meant that the shortage of ammunition had become critical and most of the division had had no rations for 24 hours or more. MacKenzie returned to the division having met with General Thomas of 43rd Division, Horrocks and Browning, and having been assured that the Poles would be ferried across later that night to be followed by 130th Brigade the next afternoon or during the night of 24/25th. None of this really convinced either MacKenzie or Urquhart that there was very much ambition to be found on the south side of the river, except among Sosabowski's brigade who seemed to be getting little encouragement.

That night – or strictly speaking the following morning at 3am – an attempt was made to put a battaltion of Poles across the river, drawing them in a chain of boats connected with a signal cable which was all that was readily available in a great enough length to span the river. The cable was not suitable and broke, forcing the Poles to try and paddle against the strong current under German fire. The operation had to be abandoned at first light and only 200 Poles had been transported, many of whom were taken prisoner as they landed, having been pushed downriver of the perimeter by the current.

43. German troops on the march near Arnhem.

Operation 'Berlin' – Day Eight

With no real progress being made and the situation worsening, the evacuation is ordered

24 September

3am	Attempts to rescue the Poles result in 200 troops crossing the river, before the operation is abandoned at first light
6.05am	Urquhart is given permission to withdraw
8.08am	The evacuation plan, Operation 'Berlin' is unveiled and scheduled for nightfall

The battle was lost, but the dying continued. The Germans did not press home a major concerted attack, however the perimeter was under sustained shelling throughout the day and the casualties mounted, leaving fewer men to man the positions. Signals from Second Army reported that 43rd Division had made little progress, but that there was now a plan to launch an attack with two battalions and a bridging unit. The plan came to nothing and at 6.05am Urquhart was given permission to withdraw, the operation was to be titled 'Berlin'; at 8.08am he told General Thomas that 'Berlin' had to take place that night.

AFTER THE BATTLE

The arrival of the Poles at Driel did little to ease the plight of the men at Oosterbeek due to the lack of boats, though reinforcing the perimeter would not have changed the tactical approach of the Germans, who were content to contain the airborne troops. They were short of infantry themselves and needed to focus on preventing, or at least delaying, the advance of XXX Corps. If that could be achieved, Urquhart's men could be defeated by shelling and starvation. They did not have the supplies to fight a defensive battle indefinitely nor the manpower to attack – and if they did achieve a breakout there was really nowhere for them to go. Reinforcement of the perimeter was a possibility. On 20 September, Major General Hakewill Smith, commander of 52nd Division offered to take the risk of leading one brigade to Arnhem in a glider descent, despite their complete lack of glider training. Browning rejected his suggestion, sending a signal that read 'Thanks for the message, but offer not, repeat not, required as situation better than you think'. It seems unlikely that the proposed brigade landing could possibly have taken place in less than 48 hours, by which time the Market Garden operation had clearly failed, but it is difficult to see how Browning could have thought the situation was anything other than dire; the main objective had not been achieved, the force which had held the north end of the bridge with such incredible determination

44. War correspondents of the Airborne Division.

had been overrun and the Airborne Dvision as a whole had been reduced to a point where any renewed attempt to fulfil its mission would have been quite impossible due to their losses, the shortage of ammunition and the sheer exhaustion of the troops. The situation clearly was not 'better' than Major General Hakewill Smith had thought.

The German language has many excellent technical terms for military situations and practices, and by the time Hakewill Smith made his offer, one of these terms was already applicable at Oosterbeek. It had become a 'kessel' or cauldron, which means a pocket of the enemy; a force which is surrounded, but still fighting. If the force cannot escape such a position by attacking, it must either surrender or evacuate by stealth.

Urquhart's evacuation plan was inspired by the withdrawal from Gallipoli in 1915, an operation he had studied in detail for an examination before the war. Each of the units was to withdraw

ROYAL ARMY CHAPLAIN'S DEPARTMENT

No department of the Airborne Division suffered a
heavier proportional loss than the Royal Army Chaplain's
Department, which is, perhaps, an inevitable consequence
of the battlefield role of the padre. Of the dozen chaplains
who served at Arnhem and Oosterbeek, two were killed in
the battle and all of the remainder, several of whom were
wounded, volunteered to remain with the casualties when
the division was evacuated.

through the night following tapes and directed by guides down to
the river, leaving medical staff and the chaplains, who volunteered
to stay and look after the wounded. The last of the ammunition
was destroyed and the breechblocks of the guns were removed
and thrown in the river. Fortunately a heavy downfall of rain and
concentrated shelling from XXX Corps artillery helped to cover
the noise and led the Germans to think that the activity at the
riverside was the arrival of reinforcements and supplies, rather than
the escape of the division. Indeed, they were not in a great hurry
to investigate since their policy was more a matter of shelling the
perimeter out of existence than making costly attacks now that the
battle was effectively over.

The retreating troops were met by boats crewed by a company of
Canadian engineers, who, despite their heroic and strenuous efforts,
could not hope to transport all of the exhausted soldiers queuing
patiently on the river bank. Some of the men stripped off and swam,
though doubtless many drowned due to the strong current and the
fact that they were already utterly exhausted. Dawn put an end to
the operation and some were left behind, but more than 2,000 men
had been successfully extracted.

All of the British commanders, Montgomery, Horrocks, Browning
and Thomas, had agreed that it was time to abandon the operation,

45. *Airborne medic at the temporary grave of Private Edmond of 1st Airlanding Reconnaissance Squadron.*

though there was another possible option that could have been attempted. General Sosabowski had proposed a plan for an assault crossing a few kilometres to the west of the perimeter where there was very little opposition and where the banks of the river were somewhat easier to negotiate. Once across the river, XXX Corps would build a bridge suitable for tanks, Urquhart's troops would be relieved from the west and the strategic objectives of Market Garden could be pursued, but it seems that everyone had lost confidence in the operation; the plan had failed and there was little interest in saving it. Shamefully, within a very short time, senior British officers were claiming Sosabowski's suggestion as their own and, worse still, suggested that the operation could have gone ahead had it not been for Sosabowski's refusal to cooperate.

Every defeat begs for an explanation and there are some contributory factors to the failure of the Arnhem operation. On balance, the operation as a whole was probably too ambitious, though the potential gains were sufficient to justify the attempt.

The first barrier to success was that the drop was much too far from the target; the element of surprise was lost and the troops assigned to the main objective had to fight their way through woods and built-up areas; a process which exhausted the men and their ammunition. Urquhart's division was delivered to the target area in three separate lifts and he was therefore never going to be able to concentrate his troops adequately unless the Germans either somehow failed to notice thousands of parachutists and hundreds of gliders landing between Wolfheze, Heelsum and Oosterbeek or decided 'en masse' to head home to Germany. Neither of these things was going to happen.

The force available on the first day of the operation was not large enough for the tasks allotted. Even if all of 1st Parachute Brigade had been able to concentrate around the bridge without incurring serious losses, they would still have been subject to the pressures that go beyond the actions of the enemy – lack of food and water. Additionally, the Germans would have been able to surround the area and concentrate their superior artillery on the brigade rather than being forced to fight near-continuous actions in the woods and streets between Arnhem and Oosterbeek.

It was all very well to plan for lifts on three successive days, but the plan took no account of possible changes in weather conditions. Realistically, there is little likelihood that even if 4th Brigade and the balance of the divisional assets had arrived at 10am on the 18th as planned, that the operation would have been any more successful, nor that dropping the Polish battalions on the 19th would have turned the course of the battle. The staging of the lifts also produced other problems. Had the division been delivered in its entirety on the 17th it would have been easier to deliver an adequate quantity of supplies on the 18th, since the transport aircraft would not have been delivering troops and there would have been sufficient force on the ground to ensure the retention of the landing zones. Most of these areas could have been abandoned to the enemy once the stores had been collected, which would have freed up units for other duties. The successive lifts also imposed a 'no-fly' policy which impeded the RAF from mounting air strikes to disrupt German troop movements towards Arnhem and Nijmegen. This was certainly a cause of contention on the ground, as the struggle at the bridge and at the Oosterbeek perimeter was not as well supported as it might have been; however, Urquhart was:

> ... naturally disturbed by the non-arrival of Horrocks's Corps, I was much more annoyed at the disappointingly meagre air support we were receiving. The resupply boys' gallantry had been magnificent, but the fighters were rare friends. We needed the Typhoons and the Tempests to carry out rocket attacks on the Germans' gun and mortar positions.

> R.E. Urquhart, *Arnhem*

Communication failures at all levels had a huge impact. Inability to communicate with the different headquarters on the continent and in England made it impossible to change the allotted zones for reinforcements and replenishment or to arrange tactical air support. The radio equipment within the division was utterly inadequate and made it impossible to coordinate the initial push into Arnhem. Communications within units were not that much better, though one officer, Digby Tatham Warter, had wisely made provision for this by training his company to respond to bugle calls; an initiative which worked extremely well.

The plan also under-rated the abilities of the enemy in two crucial aspects. Although there was ample intelligence to indicate the presence of a considerable number of first-rate combat troops within a short distance of the target, that information was not properly utilised and the capacity of the German Army and SS to react quickly and effectively under pressure was more or less ignored despite the experience of North Africa, Italy and Normandy.

Additionally, there were shortcomings in both divisional and brigade training. There had only been one divisional exercise and that had not involved dropping the troops from the air and was therefore of limited value. The high incidence of absenteeism and of men wanting to return to their units had had a disruptive effect on training and morale. Many of the units acted or responded rather slowly and some were what General Urquhart called 'bullet shy' on the first day, though this was probably an inevitable consequence of the fact that airborne troops cannot be introduced to the battle gradually – they are likely to be in the thick of it immediately and have no opportunity to acclimatise.

There seems to have been no appetite to adjust the initial plan in light of changing circumstances, but allowance should have been made for this from day one – if only because the first lift might have found that the landing zones were utterly unsuitable for gliders.

The most obvious losers at Arnhem were the men of the 1st Airborne Division and the people of Arnhem and Oosterbeek. Many civilians were killed or wounded and many more suffered from emotional distress for decades afterwards. Huge numbers of homes and businesses were destroyed or damaged and the whole population was forcibly evacuated by the Germans after the battle.

Urquhart's division, nearly 10,000 strong, was utterly ruined. More than 1,700 men were killed in the fighting; more than 6,000 were taken prisoner, and many more would die of their wounds in the months and years to come. The Polish Parachute Brigade suffered casualties in pursuit of an operation that many people considered was already lost and which took place at a critical moment for their own country. General Sosabowski and the Polish Government in exile had hoped to have the brigade committed at home in such a way as to make a political presence in the wake of the German retreat and before the Russians established a favourable administration. This was probably never a realistic proposition. Even if the British and the Americans had been prepared to transport the Poles, they would have shied away from upsetting their Russian ally. A round trip would have been beyond the range of the aircraft and there is no reason to expect that the Russians would have been willing to provide the ground facilities that would have been necessary to allow the aircraft to return to Britain. Even so, relations between the Americans, the British and the Polish Government in exile were strained by Market Garden. The British – and to a lesser extent the Americans – took the view that the Poles had received sanctuary in Britain after their defeat and should be suitably grateful. On the other hand, one has to question what was the value to Poland of providing Britain with military manpower – nearly 200,000 Poles were serving against the Germans in 1944 – if they were not going to receive a useful level of political support against the Soviet Union.

A considerable number of British and American aircrew lost their lives and a very large proportion of the aircraft committed were lost or damaged which seriously impaired the availability of air transport for some months afterwards.

The two American divisions involved experienced a great deal of hard fighting in the course of Market Garden and were then retained by Second Army for two months, during which time they were in combat almost continually. A few short weeks after they were – at last – withdrawn from the frontline, they were pitched back into the fight at Bastogne and elsewhere to obstruct the German Ardennes offensive. The Americans had not had time to rest and refit or to integrate replacements and undoubtedly suffered the more because of it.

The British Second Army was left with a long and vulnerable salient of questionable value. The flanks of the salient effectively forced the British to maintain 62 miles (100km) or more of frontline with troops who could have been more usefully employed elsewhere or who could have been resting and refitting after the strains of the battles of the previous months. This salient could not be abandoned since that would give the Germans a second victory, and would have a consequent cost in terms of morale both in the army and at home, and might also harm public perception in the United States; it would look like the British had sacrificed American lives to gain a piece of territory which they promptly handed back to the Germans. It might also cause damage to civilian confidence

131

in German-occupied Europe. There was little benefit in being liberated if the Germans were going to be able to drive the Allied forces back out again.

The behaviour of the Germans at Arnhem was highly professional, even chivalrous at times. It is unduly cynical to see this as a product of the fear of reprisal after the war. Battlefield soldiers are fairly anonymous; few see their individual actions, and there are millions of them. Some of the Germans who had served in the East were surprised and impressed by the conduct of the British, who largely behaved in a considerate and humane manner – something which is perhaps easier to maintain in a force that has not been in continuous action for weeks and months on end. Sometimes the British were just too careful; Urquhart describes paratroopers knocking on doors to ask if they could search for Germans. A member of British 2nd Battalion commented on the behaviour of the Germans once the fighting was over:

> Several of the German tank men called out to us 'Well fought, Tommy', 'Good fight eh Tommy?' They seemed to regard war in much the same way as the British regarded football.
>
> James Sims, *Arnhem Spearhead*

As the battle progressed, medical staffs came quite close to becoming a shared asset between the opposing forces. The Germans allowed British medical staff to continue operating in St Elizabeth's Hospital and the main dressing station at the Schoonord Hotel long after both places had been captured and on more than one occasion warned the British commanders of impending attacks in the vicinity of dressing stations so that the wounded could be moved, though this was not always possible. By and large the treatment of prisoners (POWs) was humane and honourable. There were exceptions on both sides, but this is inevitable in the heat of battle. German POWs were at considerable risk from their own fire and the British really had no safer place to send them. When prisoners in the tennis courts behind the Hartenstein complained that they

46. German troops in distinctive 'pea-dot' camouflage kit taken prisoner early in the fighting. About 200 German POWs were held in the tennis courts behind the Hartenstein Hotel.

were hungry and thirsty they were roundly berated by one of their own officers who told them that the British were doing the best they could under the circumstances. Elsewhere in the battle area, savage fighting continued and local doctors, nurses and volunteers were drawn in:

> There were quite a lot of civvies about, though, helping to look after the wounded and getting them off to the hospital and into the shops and houses … The civvies were smashing. No sooner had a chap caught a packet than one of them would come along and try to bandage him up.
>
> Anonymous soldier, from Christopher Hibbert, *Arnhem*

The Germans

Most – though by no means all – battles end with a defeat and a victory. The British had suffered a defeat at Arnhem and the Germans had certainly emerged as the victors. It was not lightly won; German casualties were almost certainly much heavier than claimed, but it was a victory nonetheless. It is possible to see it as a relatively minor triumph against the overall flow of the wider campaign, but it was significant for a number of reasons.

The fighting in Normandy had cost the German Army heavily in both men and equipment, and the retreat through France and into Belgium had wreaked havoc with the command structure and the organisation of units and formations, all of which had caused considerable damage to morale, as well as to the fighting capacity of the army as a whole. The speed of the retreat had slowed markedly by the end of August, partly because of the supply problems and exhaustion of the attacking Allied forces, but also because the quality of German staff work was beginning to reassert itself, due to the high standard of the troops themselves.

47. Transport and fuel shortages forced the German Army to requisition thousands of bicycles.

After the Battle

Winning a significant tactical victory at Arnhem was a major achievement in itself given the shortages of manpower, transport and armour that the German command had to contend with. It was also a major boost to morale. The enemy had mounted a dramatic offensive which had taken the Germans by surprise; some thought had been given to the possibility of an airborne attack to seize the Arnhem Bridge and both 9th and 10th Panzer divisions had undergone some training against parachute operations generally, but there was no specific contingency plan in place. Despite this, the British had been beaten – and not just any British formation, but an elite airborne division. Naturally the German propaganda machine was not slow in making the most of this, and although many German soldiers must have thought that the war could not be won, the immediate benefit to troops in the line was incalculable.

More significantly, the British advance had ground to a halt. Horrocks' XXX Corps and the American airborne divisions had secured a good deal of territory, but the strategic picture had hardly altered. Now that the headlong retreat through France and Belgium had been arrested, the Germans had an opportunity to reorganise and refit units which, though mostly badly damaged, were still far from beaten.

The Allied bombing campaign had not brought industrial production to a standstill and the factories of the Reich were still providing the army with the arms, vehicles and ammunition required to sustain the fighting and they were still introducing new weapons. Whether or not German troops believed that the V1 and V2 attacks on London would really bring the Allies to the negotiating table was neither here nor there, the fact was that Germany was still striking the enemy. Other new weapons were coming on stream and, again, most German soldiers probably doubted that these would give them a level of battlefield superiority that would guarantee victory, but they might offer a more level playing field. Although they suffered from mechanical problems, Germany had already produced much stronger tanks with more powerful guns than the Allies and propaganda materials were already promising a new generation of even more powerful armour that would be virtually impervious to British and American tanks and anti-tank weapons. The first twin-engine jet strike aircraft – the Messerschmidt 262 was beginning to make an appearance and the ordinary soldier was not being left behind either. Plans were in motion to replace the Kar 98 with the first general-issue assault rifle, the MP44.

Most German soldiers probably realised that they would never be able to throw the British and the Americans back to the channel or the Russians back to Poland, but they might make the difference between an armistice agreement and ignominious defeat. Politically this was an impossible proposition, but that may not have been clear to the men who served in the frontline. Essentially, victory at Arnhem had kept the British out of the Reich, the V2 sites were still operable and the army had acquired a bit of breathing space.

The Neder Rhine was still seen as a vulnerable part of the front, and the German High Command ordered the complete evacuation of Arnhem in order to facilitate fortification. Tens of thousands of Netherlanders were transported eastwards and thousands of them never returned. On the day Market Garden started, the entire Netherlands railway system was closed down by a general strike which continued until the liberation. The strike certainly impeded the German logistical effort and the movement of troops and material, but it also prevented the movement of coal and produce from the countryside to the cities and the whole population suffered a cold and hungry winter.

There was now an opportunity to repair the damage of the preceding months and to bring another draft of men into the army and time to train them. Just as importantly, the Allies had shot their bolt. The Germans had gained time and the Allies had lost some. The Market Garden operation had effectively expended the only remaining strategic reserve force available to Eisenhower, Montgomery and Bradley, and not only had the Allies been stopped,

48. German Pzkw or 'Panther' tank. Although mechanically unreliable, the Panther was, when operational, vastly superior to the American Sherman and British Churchill tanks.

but they would be unable to mount another major new offensive until 1945.

The time gained allowed the Germans space to reorganise the battered formations from France, but it also gave Hitler an opportunity to plan for a counter-offensive. In the winter of 1944 he was able to concentrate a force of several divisions and hundreds of tanks – many of them the powerful Panther and Tiger models – and drive into the Allied forces through the Ardennes forest. The offensive ended in failure, and was undoubtedly a major strategic mistake. The eventual loss of men and equipment meant that the German Army was utterly crippled and was never again in a position to mount counter-offensives on a large enough scale to disrupt the Allied advance when it was renewed.

The tactical victory possibly gave Hitler a little more confidence in his commanders and vindicated his belief in the courage and resilience of the Waffen SS formations. It could be presented as an indication that the fall of Germany to the Western Allies was not imminent and perhaps helped to convince him that a counter-offensive was more viable than it really was. It may have encouraged his belief that the Allies were brittle, their 'industrial' superiority was not invincible, that their resources were not endless and that they could be beaten on the battlefield. Oddly, Hitler had opined that the 'day of the parachute soldier is over' and he was not far wrong. The later Allied Rhine Crossings would be successful, but not so ambitious and did not smack of wishful thinking. Furthermore, the Germans were more tired, less confident of any kind of end other than total defeat and had no strategic reserve since the resources wasted in the Ardennes were not available in 1945.

'Could have been' is the refrain of many failed initiatives, and the airborne operation was bedevilled by misfortune as well as mismanagement. Some aspects have been exaggerated. German acquisition of the airborne plan may have helped them hone their reaction, but the objectives were already clear, as were the likely drop zones for any reinforcements. The British had declined to land at the objective on day one, so they were unlikely to do so on day two. The Netherlands resistance man, turned double agent, known as King Kong told his German handlers that they should expect an offensive on 17 September, but he had chosen the date at random and they took no notice; his actions had no effect on the operation.

The battle of Arnhem had been won and lost days before the decision was taken to evacuate the remnants of 1st Airborne Division. Horrocks's XXX Corps had consistently made slow progress. To some extent this was a near-inevitable consequence of the nature of the terrain. The low-lying ground was soft and could only be traversed on raised roads which made the British tanks easy targets for German gunners. The urban areas were hard to deal with in the face of a resolute and increasingly confident and reorganised enemy; however, the combat environment should have been factored into the planning at every stage and clearly it was

49. XXX Corps armour moving through Eindhoven.

not. There is no obvious reason for the failure to take account of either the terrain or the abilities of the enemy. The British had been fighting the Germans for five years and there was no shortage of information about the topography.

Equally, it should be borne in mind that the Germans had similar challenges; they were often unable to site their guns in the optimum positions because of a severe shortage of all-terrain vehicles and their supply situation – which was not good before the landings – was under constant threat from the two American divisions between XXX Corps and the British airborne troops and from air strikes. The fact that there was a rail workers' strike in the Netherlands from 17 September onward and a general shortage of trucks and railway rolling stock did not help either.

The leading formation of XXX Corps, the Guards Armoured Division, was consistently far too slow. No effort was made to drive the attack through the night. The days' advances never once started at first light and it was generally midday before there was any movement at all. There were several reasons for the tardiness of the ground forces. In part it was a practice born of habit. The British Army in Europe had developed a practice of harbouring for the night. In theory this was in order to ensure that the men were fed, the tanks refuelled and ammunition distributed. In France this had been an inevitable consequence of the speed of the advance. The supply chain simply could not provide material any faster, but the situation had changed. The leading elements of the army were no longer covering distances of 18 to 30 miles (30, 40 or 50 kilometres) a day and it should have been perfectly possible to maintain the troops at the front without the massive congestion that developed in the rear of XXX Corps; all the more so given that Allied air superiority had virtually freed the logistic tail from German air strikes.

Many British writers – and some others – have blamed the demands of the American formations for the supply failures of Market Garden. It is true that Patton chose to be more active than his orders really allowed and that Bradley failed to rein him in, but it was never Eisenhower's intention to prevent the American formations from advancing. Montgomery chose to believe that Eisenhower had made the Market Garden offensive the single most important operation of the campaign, but he actually knew perfectly well that Eisenhower had told him that the advance across the Rhine and into northern Germany was *a* priority, not *the* priority.

As it turned out, shortages of fuel, food and ammunition did not affect the advance of XXX Corps, but a shortage of infantry did. Losses over the months since Normandy had reduced some, if not most, of the infantry battalions substantially; some were effectively operating as just two companies and even they were not necessarily up to strength. The men who were left were physically and

50. A platoon of British infantry perched precariously on a Sherman tank. It might be better than walking, but the tank was likely to attract enemy fire and was therefore a hazardous means of transport as far as the infantry were concerned. (Courtesy of Tim Lynch)

6 POUNDER ANTI-TANK GUN

By the time the 6 pounder came into service in May 1942 it was already a good step behind the times and was only just up to the challenge of the lighter German tanks and armoured vehicles – the Mark III and Mark IV Panzerkampfwagen and the Stug assault guns. The heavier Tigers and Panthers could only be engaged at very short range and therefore at great risk to the gun's crew. The 6 pounder continued in service until the end of the war and something in the region of fifty were deployed at Arnhem, a number of others being lost en route.

emotionally exhausted. Committing them to a major new offensive where the time factor was so critical was simply unreasonable. The scarcity of infantry was a problem for the equally exhausted armoured units. Tanks without infantry are extremely vulnerable in close terrain. The tanks needed the infantry to clear the towns and woodland areas or they would suffer accordingly.

Again, this should have been a consideration in planning and the fact that it clearly was not is a measure of the unreasonably optimistic – even rash – approach to the whole operation. Once it became clear that there was no prospect of moving the Airborne Division to the bridge as originally planned, Urquhart's hands were tied. His only option was to form a perimeter and try to hold on until the arrival of XXX Corps. The suggestion that he should have concentrated his forces and thrown them bodily into the battle does not bear examination. Less than half of his troops were infantrymen. The heavy losses incurred by 1st and 4th Parachute brigades could not possibly be offset by divisional troops operating in an infantry role. From an early stage in the battle most divisional troops were fighting as infantry – including the glider pilots, who, unlike their American counterparts, were given infantry training and were expected to take a combat role on the battlefield. The divisional

51. The British 17 pounder anti-tank gun was a match for even the best German armour, but only sixteen were supplied to the anti-tank units of 1st Airborne Division. (Courtesy of Tim Lynch)

troops gave tremendous service in defence, but naturally these men did not have the same level of infantry skills as the paratroopers and the Airlanding troops and would not have fared well in the street fighting for which even the infantry element had not had sufficient training.

Urquhart's anti-tank weapons were also not adequate in either quality or quantity to take on a major armoured force in defence let alone in attack. The light 6 pounder gun was powerful enough to deal with the German armoured cars, half tracks and the lighter tanks, but not the Panthers, Tigers or the heavier self-propelled guns. The 17 pounders that could deal with such opposition were far too few in number and both weapons were very vulnerable to small arms fire and shelling.

Urquhart lost the battle on the ground, and it might appear that his career was lost as well. He did not get another combat command but since the war was coming to an end, there was probably no command to give him.

   Browning's conduct throughout the Market Garden operation –
and in fact throughout the existence of 1st Airborne Division and
1st Airborne Army – left a great deal to be desired. His wish to
have – or at least be seen as having – an active command role in
the biggest war in history is surely understandable. His failure to
do everything in his power to ensure that the troops under his
command were given a realistic task and that they were properly
trained, equipped and supported, is not. His insistence that his
own headquarters be flown to the continent when there was
a serious shortage of transport aircraft for combat troops is
incomprehensible as well as unforgiveable. Browning, like Urquhart,
was one of the losers in the sense that he never had another
significant job. Montgomery let it be known that he would be
happy to have Browning as a corps commander but no position
arose and it may be that Montgomery was simply making a noise
to protect his protégé and therefore his own reputation as a judge
of command material. Through a mixture of factors – but chiefly
collegiate protection at the time and unduly generous treatment by
historians – Browning's reputation has largely survived.

   Horrocks was far from well at the time of Market Garden and did
not perform to his usually high standards. His health did not improve
and he was forced to go back to Britain on sick leave. After the war
he became famous for his television lectures on various battles and
campaigns, including Market Garden.

   Montgomery continued to lead 21st Army Group until the end
of the war, though his position was not always as secure as it might
seem. He managed to offend and irritate Eisenhower, an unusually
considerate and diplomatic man, and undoubtedly resented the fact
that he had not been entrusted with supreme command for the
whole of the campaign in Europe.

THE LEGACY

Market Garden cast doubt on the professional competence of several senior British officers, though, in the interests of maintaining the appearance of good relations between the Allies and for the benefit of both civilian and military morale, a veil was quietly drawn across a number of factors and a quiet campaign to shift blame was staged. Some of the men whose actions were most questionable, principally Browning and Thomas, did what they could to imply that Sosabowski had let the side down when in fact he had conducted himself as a true professional in every way. He proposed a very practical operation to make a bridgehead to the west of the Oosterbeek perimeter and thus relieve the Airborne Division. The British commanders promptly claimed the plan as their own, and then equally promptly – and inexplicably – abandoned the idea completely.

The traditional conversation-filler of the British – the weather – was held responsible as well, which helped to divert attention from the failures of human beings, though the impact of the weather would have been negligible if the airborne troops had been delivered in two lifts on 17 September, not spread over three days. It did no harm that throughout the war the media – especially in Britain – were not as critical as we would expect today. A few people were more realistic. In the opinion of General de Guingand, normally Montgomery's chief of staff, but who was not present at the time of Market Garden, the operation could have been successful '… if the weather had been really good, but I wouldn't like to bet on it.'

There were material consequences beyond the destruction of 1st Airborne and the damage to the two American divisions. The further exhaustion of Second Army, already badly strained by the exertions of the campaign in Normandy, had achieved nothing of real value. The massive consumption of other precious resources, the loss of aircraft and crews which reduced the potential for air supply, the creation of a degree of bad blood between the Allies would all have been acceptable if the operation had been a success. Instead, the Allies were unable to maintain much pressure on the front and the Germans were able to stabilise their army to a considerable degree.

Beyond the drama and romance of a glorious defeat that has probably generated more interest than any other Second World War action of a comparable scale, perhaps the major legacy for Britain is the continued existence of the Parachute Regiment. There were many parachute and glider-borne operations between 1940 and 1945, varying in scale from the insertion of small numbers of men to seize or destroy a specific asset such as the German attack on Eben Emael or the Bruneval raid, to the massive landings in Crete, Normandy and Market Garden. Some were more successful than others, but all of them came at a heavy cost in casualties and this was to be expected and was, generally speaking, considered acceptable if the prize justified the risk and, naturally, if the operation was successful.

All the same, there was always a certain amount of internal army opposition to the formation of specialist airborne forces and a good deal of reluctance on the part of the RAF to diverting resources to deliver the troops to the target. The root of army opposition lay in a traditional distrust of what many senior officers saw as 'private armies' – often under the command of flamboyant leaders. For good or ill, these are very often the sort of initiatives that appeal to political leaders who are inclined to look for 'silver bullet' solutions to all sorts of challenges. More than two hundred years ago Benjamin Franklin asked how any prince could defend his realm against the sudden descent of a few thousand soldiers from the sky. Any professional soldier of the day could have told Franklin that the prince did not need to prevent those soldiers from landing; he just needed to be able to deploy his own army to surround them and starve them out. As a political thinker, Franklin did not need to think about the consequences of dropping men to take a target; he just needed to imagine the target. That is the great barrier to a parachute operation – ensuring that the force can be relieved or extracted once the objective is achieved. If the force cannot be deployed with a realistic prospect of both success and extraction, it is as much a white elephant as a silver bullet.

In the aftermath of Market Garden many senior officers, most military theorists and some politicians raised questions and expressed grave doubts about the value of airborne operations on a grand scale. Their doubts were silenced by the success of the Rhine Crossings, but the biggest questions went unanswered.

The cost of maintaining an airborne force with all of the specialist training and equipment and the way it drains the fittest, most committed and most intelligent infantry recruits from the main force battalions can only be justified if a suitably large fleet of aircraft is kept in being. No government has been able or willing to make that investment, and even if they could, a gigantic air fleet would be far too vulnerable in a modern military environment.

The tremendous courage and endurance of 1st Airborne Division made more of an impression on the public in 1944 than the fact that the operation was a complete failure; this is still the case today. At any time since Market Garden it would have been political suicidal for a government to suggest disbanding the Parachute Regiment.

Many of the reasons for the failure of Market Garden were played down or simply ignored in the weeks and months after the campaign for a mixture of reasons, stretching from understandable

GENERAL URQUHART

General Urquhart visited Arnhem and Oosterbeek
after the war and was surprised and delighted at the
warm welcome he received from the community;
he had rather expected that there would be some
resentment over the loss of life and the destruction of
property. General Urquhart located a suitable site for
the Airborne War Cemetery near Oosterbeek and was
instrumental in founding the annual Arnhem pilgrimage.

concerns about security and public perceptions to the protection
of the reputation of command structure, formations, units and
specific individuals. The operation had suffered from poor planning
in general and poor communication and coordination between
the relevant headquarters and commanders. The drop and landing
zones were far too far from the targets and too many objectives
were assigned to forces that were too small for their tasks. In his
own book, General Urquhart stresses the important point that an
airborne division is designed to be deployed as a division, not as
a collection of units delivered to the battlefield in three lifts over
three days.

Failure was not simply a matter of fighting with a reduced force
for the early stages of the operation, though that clearly was very
significant. Inevitably the first units in action – most particularly the
1st Parachute Brigade – would bear the brunt of the casualties in the
early stages of the fight. They would also have to march more than
6 miles (10km) measured across the map; however, infantry seldom
get to travel as the crow flies. Roads are seldom straight and the
enemy cannot be relied on to avoid combat. Between fighting and
marching, 1st Brigade was bound to be tired by the end of the first
day even if resistance was light. Consequently they would be less fit
for battle on the second and subsequent days and would therefore

be a declining asset, less capable of contributing to a second push onto Arnhem by the units arriving on the 18th in the event of the first attack failing to attain the objectives of the operation. It would seem that little, if any, thought was given to such an eventuality. Seemingly there was no 'plan B', or if there was, that plan had not been clearly explained to Hicks, Lathbury or Hackett.

The information available on the eve of an attack always requires a degree of sifting. Intelligence analysis is not an exact science. Planners must make judgements about the accuracy of intelligence material and commanders have to make judgements about its significance and then incorporate the intelligence into their plan to the best of their ability. Commanders never have a complete picture of the enemy's strength, combat readiness or morale, let alone a perfect understanding of the terrain; geographical features that are too small to feature on a map may have a tremendous bearing on some tiny action on which, unexpectedly, has a major influence on the course of the wider battle.

The intelligence indications that were passed to General Urquhart suggested that the German forces available for the defence of Arnhem and for the reaction to the airborne landings were fairly limited, but they were not non-existent – or even negligible. Even on the most optimistic analysis there were numerous armoured vehicles. British commanders were aware that the 6 pounder anti-tank guns on issue to most troops of the Royal Artillery Airlanding anti-tank batteries and to the infantry battalions of 1st Airlanding Brigade were less than adequate and it should have been expected that the Germans would deploy whatever armour they could find as quickly as they could, secure in the knowledge that the parachute formations would struggle to neutralise them.

German forces in and around the operational area were considerably greater than Urquhart's information suggested, and it should have been expected that the German commanders would react quickly and with efficiency. The battle was to take place on the very doorstep of the Reich so they would be sent every possible

52. A 6 pounder anti-tank gun moving towards Arnhem in the early stages of the operation. Failures in training and doctrine would lead to the loss of many anti-tank guns during the battle.

resource as quickly as possible. Even if the assessment of armoured vehicles in the vicinity had been correct, given the enterprise and daring in the Germans' use of light armour in Normandy, their actions on the first day at Arnhem should not have come as a surprise to the British, and a second 'push' towards the bridge should therefore have figured in both the 1st Parachute Brigade plan and in the divisional plan.

The fact that Hicks was obliged to form a reserve to intervene in support of 1st Brigade by stripping troops from his own Airlanding Brigade and Hackett's 4th Parachute Brigade indicates that there had been an unreasonable level of confidence in the capacities of the three parachute battalions committed to seizing the objectives on the first day of the operation. Although the operation as a whole was a failure, it is worth bearing in mind that in the strictest sense the attempt to take the main objective – Arnhem Bridge, was more or less achieved despite the distance from the objective, the heavier resistance of the Germans, the communications problems and the utter failure to put the Reconnaissance Squadron onto the target at all, let alone in the time frame that Urquhart and his staff had envisaged.

Frost was unable to secure the objective in its entirety, and even if the whole of 1st Parachute Brigade had reached the target by the close of 17 September it is by no means clear that they would have been able to take the south end of the bridge. The Germans tried to force a crossing on the morning of the 18th. They mounted an attack in considerable strength with artillery and armoured support but were stopped in their tracks.

Although they were unable to secure the whole bridge, the force based on 2nd Battalion was able to deny its use to the enemy and prevent its demolition; they also held their position for a longer period than the planners had thought would be necessary. Whatever the failings in the planning or execution of Market Garden as a whole; Frost's mixed force of parachute infantry and men of the Royal Army Service Corps, the Royal Engineers, Royal Artillery and the Glider Pilot Regiment, and all of the medics, doctors and chaplains, had more than done their job.

If there is a positive enduring legacy to Market Garden it lies in the performance of the officers and men of the Airborne Division; not just at what is now called the John Frost Bridge, but across the battlefield as a whole. The failure to reinforce Frost was not due to a lack of commitment or skill. The initial attack could and should have been better planned, but in the end the paratroopers and glider infantry of 1st Airborne were defeated by an equally determined enemy in greater numbers and with greater armoured support than the airborne forces could ever have been expected to deal with. On the first day of Market Garden, the German Commander Bittrich had warned his officers that the British would be 'incredible in defence'; the conduct of the airborne forces, from Arnhem Bridge to the Oosterbeek cauldron, and the landing and drop zones of Ginkel Heath, amply proved his opinion to be correct.

53. A Sherman tank at the entrance to the Airborne Museum, formerly the Hartenstein Hotel, Oosterbeek. (Author photograph)

ORDERS OF BATTLE

1st British Airborne Division and 1st Polish Parachute Brigade

Divisional headquarters

General Office Commanding (GOC), Major General R.E. Urquhart, DSO
Urquhart's ADC, Captain G.C. Roberts
Urquhart's senior staff officer, Lieutenant Colonel C.B. MacKenzie
Staff Officers, Major Newton-Dunn, Major Madden and Major Maguire, Lieutenant Colonel Preston, Major Hardman and Major Hodges
HQ Royal Artillery (RA), Lieutenant Colonel Loder-Symonds and Major Tower
HQ Royal Engineers (RE), Lieutenant Colonel Myers and Captain Green
Divisional Signals, Lieutenant Colonel Stephenson and Major Deane-Drummond
HQ Royal Army Service Corps, Lieutenant Colonel Packe and Major Clark
Royal Army Medical Corps (RAMC), Colonel Warrack and Major Miller

Royal Army Ordnance Corps (RAOC), Lieutenant Colonel Mobbs
Royal Electrical and Mechanical Engineers (REME), Captain Ewens
Royal Army Chaplaincy Department (RAChD), Major Harlow
Provost Marshal, Major Haig

1st Parachute Brigade (Brigadier Lathbury)

Brigade Major Hibbert and DAA/QMG Major Byng-Maddick.
1st Battalion Parachute Regiment (Lieutenant Colonel Dobie)
2nd Battalion Parachute Regiment (Lieutenant Colonel Frost)
3rd Battalion Parachute Regiment (Lieutenant Colonel Fitch)
1st Parachute Reconnaissance Squadron (less one troop to be retained as Divisional Reserve), (Major Gough)

3rd Airlanding Light Battery, RA (Major Munford)

1st Airlanding Anti-Tank Battery, RA (Major Arnold)

1st Parachute Squadron, RE (Major Murray)

16th Parachute Field Ambulance RAMC (Lieutenant Colonel Townsend)

Detachment RASC

4th Parachute Brigade (Brigadier Hackett)

Brigade Major Dawson

156th Battalion Parachute Regiment (Lieutenant Colonel des Voeux)

10th Battalion Parachute Regiment (Lieutenant Colonel Smyth)

11th Battalion Parachute Regiment (Lieutenant Colonel Lea)

2nd Airlanding Light Battery, RA (Major Linton)

2nd Airlanding Anti-Tank Battery, RA (Major Haynes)

4th Parachute Squadron, RE (Major Perkins)

133rd Parachute Field Ambulance, RAMC (Lieutenant Colonel Alford)

Detachment RASC

1st Airlanding Brigade (Brigadier Hicks)

Deputy Commander, Colonel Barlow, Brigade Major Blake

1st Battalion Border Regiment (Lieutenant Colonel Hadden)

7th Battalion King's Own Scottish Borderers (KOSBs), (Lieutenant Colonel Payton-Reid)

2nd Battalion South Staffordshires (Lieutenant Colonel McCardie)

1st Airlanding Light Battery, RA (Major Walker)

181st Field Ambulance, RAMC (Lieutenant Colonel Marrable)

Detachment, RASC

Divisional Troops

HQ of 1st Light Regiment RA, (Lieutenant Colonel Thompson) – the three batteries of the regiment were initially assigned to the three brigades of the division

No. 1 Forward Observation Unit (Major Wight-Boycott)

9 Field Company, RE (Major Winchester)

21st Independent Parachute Company (Major Wilson)

No. 1 Wing, Glider Pilot Regiment (Lieutenant Colonel Murray)

No. 2 Wing, Glider Pilot Regiment (Lieutenant Colonel Place)

250 Light Company and 93rd Company, RASC

Divisional Provost Company (Captain Gray)

In addition, the divisional troops included detachments from REME workshops and RAOC parks with responsibility for the maintenance of divisional transport and the administration of the divisional ammunition supply.

1st Polish Parachute Brigade (Major General Sosabowski)

Deputy Commander, Lieutenant Colonel *Jachnick*

1st Polish Parachute Battalion (Lieutenant Colonel Tonn)

2nd Polish Parachute Battalion (Lieutenant Colonel Ploszewski)

3rd Polish Parachute Battalion (Major Sobocinski), (the 3rd Battalion was eventually dropped near Grave on 23 September)

Medical Company (Lieutenant Mozdzierz)

Engineers Company (Captain Budziszewski)

Transport and Supply Company (Captain Siudzinski)

Anti-Tank Battery (Captain Wardzala)

The Germans

The German Order of Battle for the Arnhem operation is, naturally, much less clear than that of the Allied forces. Numerous 'units' were ad hoc conglomerations of men from any and all branches of the army, navy and air force swept up from the vicinity and committed to the fight.

Such records as survived are not all complete and can be very misleading. A list of unit titles would show several armoured and artillery units that had neither guns nor tanks and whose men served as infantry throughout the battle. Several of the units that did bring armour to the fight were seriously understrength and at least one was equipped with a handful of French Renault tanks captured in 1940, which had been retained for training purposes and were hardly suitable for frontline duty by the standards of 1944.

Major Kershaw (*It Never Snows in September*, 1990) has painstakingly constructed a sort of 'schematic flow diagram' to show the arrival and deployments of German forces throughout the entire Market Garden area of operations. Major Kershaw's diagrams would indicate that something like 10,000 German troops were committed to actions in the Arnhem/ Oosterbeek/Wolfheze area between 17 and 26 September. Although there were initially two armoured divisions in the Arnhem/Velp area, both were very weak in men and vehicles. Additionally, only one of these formations (9th SS Panzer) was committed to the Arnhem battle, the other (10th SS Panzer) being dispatched to Nijmegen. In total, it is probably reasonable to see the German forces as being the rough equivalent of an armoured division, perhaps with a rather stronger artillery element. However, the initial German deployment can be conveniently split in to two forces deployed to the east and west of 1st Airborne Division. The below is a high-level guide to the composition of these forces:

9th SS Panzer Division (Lieutenant Colonel Walther Harzer)

The Eastern force amounted to something less than 3,000 men from the combat elements of 9th Panzer

Division were available in the Arnhem area on 17 September consisted of:

9th SS Panzer Regiment (who had no tanks and fought as infantry)

19th SS Infantry Regiment

20th SS Infantry Regiment
9th SS Divisional Reconnaissance
  Unit (with about 30 light armoured
  vehicles)
9th SS Artillery (who had no guns and
  fought as infantry)
SS Panzer Jager (Tank destroyer)
  Battalion (who had no vehicles and
  fought as infantry)
9th SS Anti-Aircraft and 9th SS
  Engineering Battalion were available
  but were stationed at Deelen and
  Brummen respectively

To the west, the Division von
  Tettau – purely an administrative
  formation – was quickly reorganised
  as a battlegroup through the night of
  17–18 September and consisted of:

6/14 Naval Manning Battalion
184th Artillery Regiment who had no
  guns and fought as infantry
SS Wach Battalion 'Helle'
SS Battalion 'Schulz'
SS Lippert NCO training unit
SS Battalion 'Mattusch'
SS Battalion 'Oelkers'
SS Battalion 'Eberwein'
Battle group 'Knoche'
SS NCO training unit 'Kraft' was
  transferred to the Spindler Battle
  group by midnight of the 17th.
Battlegroup '3 Holland Airfield Area'
Panzer Company 224 (a training unit
  with about 15–17 tanks, mostly
  obsolete Renaults)

Kampfgruppen/ Battlegroups

In addition to the two divisonal formations, a variety of ad hoc battlegroups were formed as troops were brought into the battle area. The composition of these formations changed continually as units and sub-units of different formations were added or removed depending on the tasks in hand or on the needs of other operations, whether around Arnhem/Oosterbeek or further afield; units from 9th SS Panzer of Division 'Tettau' passed from one battlegroup to another as the situation required. Additionally, many units, some of them very small, were formed from scattered parties from a wide range of sources which were allocated to battlegroups in a piecemeal fashion. German records are, understandably, incomplete, but the following units – or elements of them – were committed to the battle at different times:

21st SS Panzergrenadier Regiment
506th Heavy Tank Battalion
280th Assault Gun Brigade
20th SS Panzergrenadier Regiment

FURTHER READING

Bennet, D., *A Magnificent Disaster* (Casemate Books, 2008)

Buckingham, William, *Arnhem 1944* (Tempus/The History Press, 2002)

Clark, Lloyd, *Arnhem: Operation Market Garden, September 1944* (Sutton/The History Press, 2002)

Fairley, J., *Remember Arnhem. The Story of the 1st Airborne Reconnaissance Squadron at Arnhem* (Pegasus Journal, 1978)

Frost, J., *A Drop Too Many* (1980 [repr. Pen & Sword, 2008])

Heaps, L., *The Grey Goose of Arnhem* (Futura Publications, 1997)

Hibbert, C., *Arnhem* (Batsford, 1962)

Horrocks, B., *A Full Life* (Leo Cooper, 1974)

Kent, R., *First In! Parachute Pathfinder Company* (Batsford, 1979)

Kershaw, R., *It Never Snows in September* (Crowood Press, 1990)

Middlebrook, Martin, *Arnhem 1944: The Airborne Battle* (Penguin Books, 1995)

Powell, G., *The Devil's Birthday* (Ashford, Buchan & Enright, 1984)

Sims, James, *Arnhem Spearhead: A Private Soldier's Story* (Imperial War Museum, 1978)

Urquhart, R.E., *Arnhem* (Cassell & Co., 1958)

Waddy, J., *A Tour of the Arnhem Battlefields* (Pen & Sword, 1990)

The internet is a fantastic resource for discovering more about Arnhem, some recommended websites are:

www.airbornemuseum.nl

www.defendingarnhem.com

www.pegasusarchive.org

INDEX

Index